COTSWOLD WALKS

A winter's day at Bourton-on-the-Water (Walk 10)

Cotswold Walks
Book 2: Central Region

by
Clive Holmes

CICERONE PRESS
MILNTHORPE, CUMBRIA

© Clive Holmes 1993
ISBN 1 85284 140 0
A catalogue record for this book is available from the British Library.

DEDICATION
For Deb and Nick

ACKNOWLEDGEMENTS

The preparation of this series of Cotswolds Walks has been a long process, it has also been a most interesting and enriching one but without the help of others it might not have reached fruition.

I would like to thank my wife for her constructive advice about routes and places of interest, for her administrative help and above all for her company on each of the sixty walks, in all weathers. Further, my thanks are also due to all members of my family and to those friends as well who joined us for some of the walks in the northern region.

Finally I must pay tribute to the surgical team, the nursing staff and to the physiotherapists of Luton and Dunstable Hospital, Bedfordshire, who worked so hard to give me back the use of my damaged fingers of my right-hand shortly after the commencement of this work. I will always be grateful!

Clive Holmes

Front cover: The Mill at Lower Slaughter
Photo: Malcolm Holmes.

CONTENTS

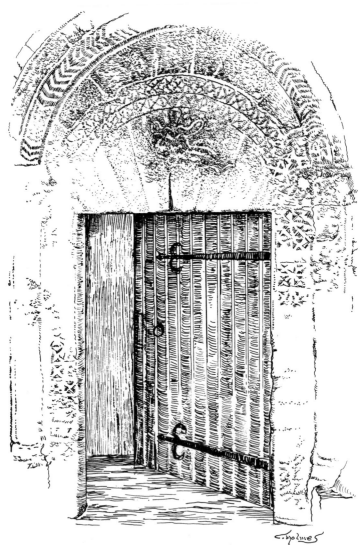

The unfinished carving of the Tree of Life above the Norman doorway.
The church of St Mary the Virgin, Lower Swell (Walk 1)

INTRODUCTION

The History of the Region

> "I praise God and ever shall
> It is the sheep hath paid for it all"

So reads the inscription on a Cotswolds merchant's house: an accurate and enlightened summary of the reasons for the Cotswold's development and the survival of the region in its present form, untarnished by industry and characterised by a wealth of beautiful landscapes and settlements rich in history and character. A walkers paradise indeed.

The area that we know today as the Cotswolds became rich over the past generations thanks to sheep farming and in particular to the local breed of sheep known as The Cotswold, each of which, it was said, could produce 28lb of fleece. With the passage of time mills sprang up in the valleys, where the rivers provided power for the manufacture of cloth, thus increasing the wealth of the region.

In the early days the sheep's fleece was exported to Europe to be woven. However, during the reign of Edward III it became apparent that the English would do better to both produce *and* weave the fleece. Flemish weavers were persuaded to emigrate to England, thus the wool industry was founded. From that point on trade rapidly flourished and in time came to dominate the economy.

At its peak the area known as the Cotswolds was producing over half of the total national wool product, so great had become the capacity of the area. Half of the local population were employed in some part of the woollen cloth production process and the area grazed over half a million sheep. The region as a whole was very comfortably off, but it was the merchants and the dealers who profited enormously, so much so that they were able to lend money to the Exchequer and to build fine houses, develop their estates and put vast amounts of money into their local churches.

Unfortunately, this happy state of affairs did not last forever and whilst other parts of Britain were developing and prospering during the industrial revolution, the Cotswolds generally went into a decline. Many of the mills closed and whole villages fell into ruin. Families moved out of the area, the men folk seeking employment

7

in newer industries in other parts of the country.

Consequently, the effects of the Industrial Revolution, which had brought about profound changes upon the landscape in other areas of the country, left the Cotswolds largely unscathed. It is thanks to this rapid decline in the prosperity of the area during the eighteenth and early nineteenth centuries that the Cotswolds remains today a region of rolling English countryside, interrupted at intervals by villages and towns characterised by a wealth of architecture which is pleasant and acceptable to the eye: ancient, undisturbed churches, rows of irregular cottages and the fine houses in acres of parkland built by the once wealthy merchants.

The name Cotswolds well describes the area as a whole. The word "wold" meant "upland common" in old English and the derivation of "Cot" is believed to have come from a word meaning an enclosure for sheep. Another theory as to the origin of the region's name is that a Saxon leader who farmed up around the source of the river Windrush had the name "Cod" pronounced "Code" and the land was known as Code's High Land. Thus, in later centuries by combination of all three we have "Cotswolds" being applied to the whole area not just to the area around the headwaters of the Windrush.

Why Walk in the Cotswolds?

The Cotswold region is certainly one of the most popular of England's designated Areas of Outstanding Natural Beauty. It has been a source of inspiration for artists who have striven to capture the feeling and atmosphere of its landscape and architecture on canvas, just as writers and poets have tried to capture its unique qualities in the verbal imagery of their poetry and prose.

During the last half century, the family car and the tour bus have allowed many visitors access to this and other parts of our country that had previously been out of reach. Many people now speed through the countryside viewing the scenery through the windows of a car or coach. They may stop for morning coffee at Bibury, a stroll around the town of Burford, lunch at Stow-on-the Wold, cream tea at Chipping Camden, and, after a dash around Broadway, they head for home having "done" the Cotswolds. Few of these people, though enchanted by what they have seen, have had the opportunity to experience the full magnitude of the beauty of the landscape through which they have been whisked. All they have seen is a fleeting glimpse of some of the most popular Cotswold towns.

This is a pity indeed, for the Cotswold region offers a wealth of opportunities to escape from the pressure and pace of the twentieth-century urban living and to retreat back into an area in which the destructive aspects of development have not left their mark.

To experience the Cotswold region fully, to learn of its history, to be enticed by its charm and to revel in its peace and beauty, one must abandon the wheel and take to one's feet.

The Cotswolds must surely have everything that makes for good and interesting walking. Although it lacks in high moorland, mountains and the drama associated with such spectacular scenery, it does have the ideal combination of ingredients for the walker who likes to discover and explore at the same time. It is a fine mix of hills, valleys, woods, farmland, water meadows, ancient tracks, paths and lanes linking picturesque villages and towns of mellow honey coloured stone. The whole region, being steeped in history, is as rich and colourful as anywhere in England.

About These Walks

The walks in these books do not confine themselves to the boundaries of the designated Cotswolds Area of Outstanding Natural Beauty. This area is covered in detail but a number of additional peripheral regions of interest are also included.

Routes suggested start at tiny Ilmington close to Shipston on Stour in the north and stretch down to Wiltshire's Castle Combe in the south. To the west the walks will take you to Stinchcombe within sight of the River Severn, whilst the area around Woodstock in Oxfordshire is also visited in the east.

In planning these walks I have endeavoured to suit all tastes, with both walking and places of interest the major objectives. Some walks have been included just for the sheer beauty of the countryside through which they pass, whilst others have been included because they give good browsing opportunities down village streets, over ancient sites or in historical churches.

Each walk has straightforward instructions: an outline route, followed by a simple and easy to follow numbered set of instructions

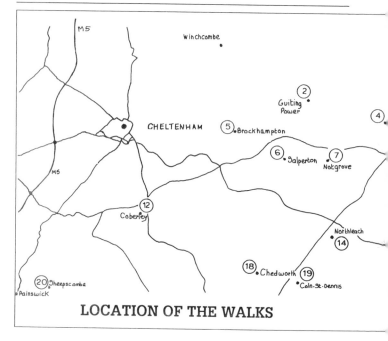

LOCATION OF THE WALKS

which tie in with a route map. All the walks detailed are circular and in most cases where I feel that clear instructions can be given for parking I have provided them. Details of Places and Points of Interest Along the Way are also given. The number of the appropriate Ordnance Survey Landranger map is given for each walk, together with the Grid Reference for the start.

The Walker's Rights on Access to the Cotswolds Paths

The right of way for the walker is along a *footpath, bridleway* or *byway*. Horseriders also have access to *bridleways*, as do pedal cyclists. The *byway* may be used by all those already mentioned with the addition of the motor vehicle. On all three you may walk your dog.

Footpaths crossing fields which have been ploughed must be made good by the farmer to a minimum width of one metre, within a maximum of two weeks. Similarly, farmers must prevent a crop

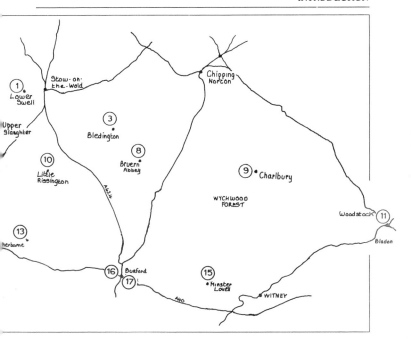

from making the path difficult to follow. Footpaths along the edges of fields are the farmer's responsibility to clear to 1.5 metres wide. If the footpath is obstructed, eg. by barbed wire, you have the right to remove sufficient of the obstruction to allow access but the matter should be reported to the highway authority and to the Ramblers' Association. Cows and horses in fields are not considered to be an obstruction to the walker, but bulls of certain breeds - British Friesian, British Holstein, Ayrshire, Dairy Shorthorn, Kerry, Jersey and Guernsey - should not be in fields through which a public footpath runs. All other bulls, unless with heifers or cows, are also banned.

When reporting any obstruction on a public right of way give the grid reference, the date and all relevant information. You may find the following address useful: Ramblers' Association, 1-5 Wandsworth Road, London, SW8 2XX (Tel: 071 582 6878).

1: Lower Swell, Upper Swell

Map Landranger:	163
Start:	GR: SP 174 257
Distance:	2½ miles

This picturesque route, linking Lower Swell to Upper Swell is along firm, level terrain and is a pleasant walk when time is short.

Route

1. Park the car by the Church of St Mary at Lower Swell. Walk down the hill, turn left then turn left again onto the main road B4068 where the sign reads Stow 1 mile.

2. Pass the Old Farmhouse Hotel on the left, the Golden Ball Inn on the right and follow the road round to the left. At the right bend turn left into the tarmacked fenced track and, ignoring the stile on the left, walk ahead.

3. After passing Bowl Farm on the right and a pair of semi-detached cottages on the left, go through the metal kissing gate left just before the notice reading "Private".

4. Once in the field the pathway bears slightly left away from the tarmacked track. Aim for the telegraph pole straight ahead to the right of the large tree and exit into the next field via a gate.

5. Walk to the end of the field close to the river and pass through a

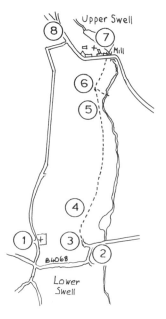

At upper Swell turn left and walk up the hill

wooden kissing gate. Continue through two more gates with metal barns ahead.

6. Eventually arrow markers indicate the way around a small field for horses. Follow the pathway between fences, with the river on the right, exiting onto the road over the stile and through a metal gate.

7. You are now at Upper Swell. Go right to admire the old bridge and the former mill, then turn and walk up the road following it round to the right, past the barns (right) and the old water faucet set into the wall (left).

8. Walk a short distance along the main road until the sign (left) to Lower Swell, The Slaughters, is reached. Follow this side road back to St Mary's Church and your car.

Places and Points of Interest Along the Way

THE SWELLS

Upper Swell and Lower Swell are situated about a mile from one another. The unusual name of these two villages is thought to have been derived from an abbreviation of "Our Ladies Well".

Upper Swell is little more than a collection of very striking Cotswold barns close to where the road crosses the River Dickler as it flows on towards Bourton-on-the-Water. The narrow bridge dates from the eighteenth century and the tiny Church of St Mary, situated close to the sixteenth-century manor house, is of Norman origin.

Lower or "Nether" Swell is the larger village and is well spread out along the road, while the Church of St Mary the Virgin overlooks the village from its high vantage point. Archaeological evidence proves that a Roman crematorium stood on this same site, as did a Saxon church in later years. Prehistoric burial mounds in the immediate vicinity clarified that the area had been one of religious

*Lower Swell is
well served with
picturesque pubs*

The church of St Mary's, Upper Swell

significance for 5,000 years. The oldest parts of today's church, however, are Norman, the most notable being the doorway, with a tympanum bearing an unfinished carving of the Tree of Life, the finely carved chancel arch and the tiny chancel itself with the Norman window on its south side. Records show that the first vicar to be appointed to the church took up his post in 1282.

During more recent times Lower Swell may well have become as popular amongst those who "took the waters" as Bath or Buxton. For during the early 1800s, between a row of ordinary Cotswold cottages on the Cheltenham to Stow road, a strange looking Spa building was developed. It was thought to have been the work of Samuel Pepys Cockerell, a well known architect of his day who re-modelled the mansion at nearby Sezincote. The tiny Spa building, with a Hindu style hood and a pineapple above the door, was probably built as a staging post where guests travelling up to Sezincote could freshen up for the journey's last stage. "Pineapple Spa" as it is known locally, has recently had its water checked for quality and much work has been carried out on its interior. Who knows, it may yet rise to a future fame to rival Bath or Buxton!

15

2: Guiting Power, Temple Guiting, Kineton

Map Landranger:	163
Start:	GR: SP 092 248
Distance:	5 miles

This is an all-weather walk being mainly over tarmac surfaces. It combines good views with hills, woods, farmland and picturesque villages, and if you choose to visit the village of Temple Guiting you may be fortunate to see some llamas on the recently established Cotswold Llama Farm situated near the large artificial lake.

Approaching Temple Guiting on a winter's day

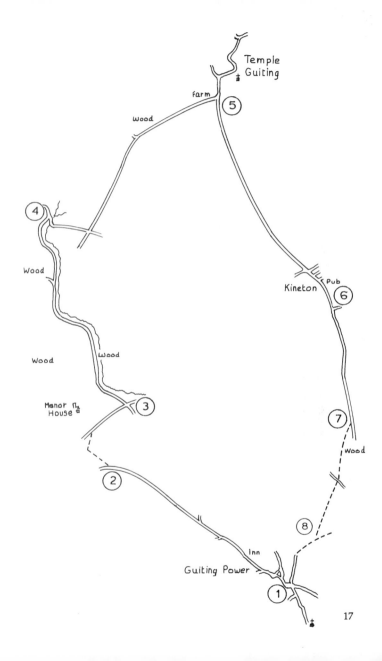

Temple
Guiting

Farm

⑤

Wood

④

Wood

Wood

Wood

Manor
House

③

②

Kineton

Pub

⑥

⑦

Wood

⑧

Inn

Guiting Power

①

17

*The church and barns
at Guiting Power*

Route

1. Park alongside the green or at the village hall towards the church at Guiting Power. Walk up the street past the Old Post Office (right). Continue up the hill and out of the village passing the Ye Olde Inn (right).

2. Continue up the hill until you reach a footpath sign (right), go over the stile and walk down the field aiming for the marker ahead in the trees. Cross the stile and walk diagonally right up the steep field towards the road passing through the gate onto the road at the sign Kineton Public Road, turn right and walk along the road.

3. On reaching the sign Unsuitable For Motors turn left and follow the track with the river down (right). At the fork go right, pass the cottage on the left and pass through the gate. Walk along the track through the woods with the river below (right) until you reach a pumping station with the notice East Worcester Waterworks.

4. Turn sharp right and climb the hill. At the crossing of the tracks go left and continue to climb towards Temple Guiting.

5. After passing through the wood, at the hill top the track descends to the edge of the village with farm buildings (left). To visit the village go left. To continue the walk go right and follow the road to Kineton which is about a mile distant.

6. Pass or pause at the Halfway House (left) then continue for about $1/2$ mile.

7. On reaching a pair of stone semi-detached cottages (left), follow the public right of way signposted right through the metal gate and turn diagonally left across the field, aiming for the right hand end of the hedge ahead.

8. Continue ahead with the hedge (left), cross the track and continue ahead with a wire fence and a young hedge (left). Walk on down the hill crossing the stiles and the footbridge as you return between the cottages to Guiting Power.

Cottages at Guiting Power

Places and Points of Interest Along the Way

GUITING POWER

Guiting Power is a typical, small Cotswold village, straggling for the most part along the western slopes of the Windrush valley, yet with attractive cottages grouped about a triangular village green as its centre. Situated at the village edge overlooking the open countryside the Church of St Michael has richly ornamented Norman doorways. The early English chancel was probably built during the twelfth century with the tower being added about 300 years later. The church was enlarged and restored during the early 1900s as it had been allowed to fall into disrepair during the late 1800s.

TEMPLE GUITING

Secluded among the tree lined banks of the Windrush, Temple Guiting acquired its name after Gilbert de Lacy gave the village to the Knights Templar during the twelfth century.

Little remains of the original twelfth-century structure of St Mary's Church owing to a succession of refurbishments over the years.

It is generally felt that the word Guiting is a derivation of the word gushing, which the River Windrush certainly does in its close proximity to both villages.

KINETON

This tiny farming hamlet is little more than a cluster of cottages beside a country lane. It is, however, a pleasant place to pass through and it has a good village pub.

Guiting Power

3: Bledington, Oddington, Maugersbury, Icomb

Map Landranger:	163
Start:	GR: SP 234 228
Distance:	9½ miles

This route, through woodland and over hill, covers some of the lesser known areas to the east and south of Stow-on-the-Wold and is partly along paths, tracks and side roads. It takes in the villages of Bledington, Lower and Upper Oddington, Maugersbury and Icomb. The track from Bledington to Lower Oddington can be very muddy. It is, therefore, recommended that this route is followed only in dry weather.

Route

1. At Bledington start from the village green in front of the Kings Head Inn and turn left walking along the road in the direction of Stow-on-the-Wold. After the last building on the right, a bungalow, take the bridleway across Heath Lane Nature Reserve, follow the track round left and over a disused railway line.

2. Continue ahead along the track for about ¼ mile when it turns sharp right, then sharp left. After about a further ⅝ mile, a sharp left is indicated by a blue arrow marker which in turn is soon followed by a sharp right. The route from here to Lower Oddington Church is a straightforward ¾ mile.

3. At the Church the track joins a lane which brings you into the village itself. With the post office right at

St Nicholas' Church, Lower Oddington

the T-junction turn left, walk through the village in the direction of Upper Oddington passing the Manor (right) and the former school with its bell still on the roof (left).

4. Continue down the hill and out of the village towards Upper Oddington. After passing the Horse and Groom on the right, note the good views across the countryside to the left at the top of this hill. At the T-junction with the B4450 from Bledington turn right and climb up Martins Hill. As you approach the main road (A436 to Stow-on-the-Wold) observe the village of Maugersbury to the left and Stow straight ahead.

5. At the A436 turn left at the Maugersbury Village Only sign. Walk up the hill into the village centre taking the first left, then left again and leave the village by descending the hill. Continue straight ahead, then left to Oxleaze Farm and at the bottom of the hill pass between the embankments that once supported a railway bridge above.

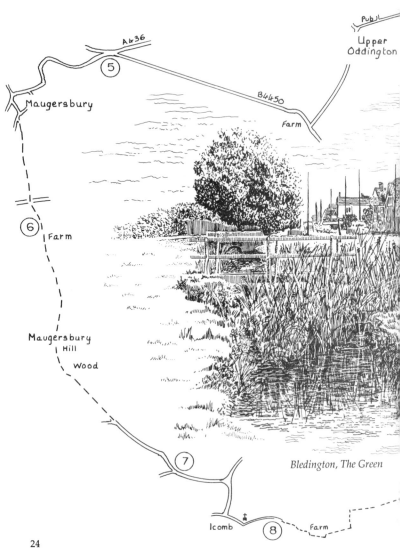

Bledington, The Green

Lower Oddington

④

Wood

③

Wood

Wood

Wood

Wood

②

Wood

Holmes

Farm

⑨

①

Pub

Bledington

arm

The Horse and Groom, Upper Oddington

The track to Oxleaze Farm

6. At the farm bear right, follow the track up the hill, pass through a metal gate and climb to the summit of Maugersbury Hill. Leaving the woods behind continue down the hill observing the distant views across the countryside.

7. Pass a signpost on the right, Little Rissington 3¼ miles, and continue to descend the hill. Pass the signpost to Icomb and turn right with Home Farm on the left to enter the village. At the village centre turn left past the phone box (right) and pass to the right of the church.

8. Pass the signpost to Bledington and Wescott, go over the stile, turn left through the farmyard and down the hill. The track runs between fields and passes further farm buildings (left). Go through a metal gate and take the footpath with the yellow marker to the left, the right of way passes through a gate in the hedge before turning right. Here the footpath skirts the field, goes over a stile and still staying to the right crosses a further stile in the facing hedge into the next field and exits through a gateway.

9. Soon you come to a track to Lower Farm (right). Cross it, stay on the footpath over the meadows, the route back to the B4450 being clearly marked from here. When you reach the road (B4450) turn right for Bledington.

The right of way at Icomb goes between the church and the barn 27

Places and Points of Interest Along the Way

BLEDINGTON

As you enter the village you cannot help being impressed by two things. One is the way the clusters of picturesque old houses sit

Icomb village

beside the village green. The other is the number of ducks that live in and around the stream that flows through the green. Bledington is a tranquil place, pleasant in its architecture and for the walker well placed beside the Oxfordshire Way.

The Church of St Leonard is well worth a visit too. A church has been here since 1150 but as usual in England various additions have been made over the centuries resulting in interesting architectural development.

The story tellers have it that much of the stained glass from the ruined Church of St Nicholas at Oddington was installed here after the battles of the Civil War.

THE ODDINGTONS and the OLD CHURCH OF ST NICHOLAS

It is thought that in pre-Saxon times "The Odyn" was the name of

the stream that flowed closed by the village church and the word "ton" meant town, by combining both over the centuries the name of Oddington has evolved. During the Civil War the village of Oddington was involved in much fighting and the Royalists under Prince Rupert were defeated here in 1643.

Much later during the Black Death the village seems to have been deserted, then rebuilt again higher up the hill. According to legend a vixen raised her cubs in the pulpit of the ruins of St Nicholas's during the 1800s, restoration only being started as late as 1912 and continuing until 1974. The chapel and aisle are the oldest part of the church and the south doorway dates from Norman times while the porch is fourteenth century. Perhaps, however, this little church's most famous attribute is the fourteenth-century "Doom Painting" on the north wall of the nave, now much faded by time, though a surprising amount of gory detail is still apparent in the artist's representation of the Last Judgement.

ICOMB

The village of Iacumbe as it was called, was mentioned in the Domesday Book as it was "owned" by St Mary's of Worcester in the County of Worcester; not until 1844 did Icomb become part of Gloucestershire.

Due to the fact that Icomb was something of an island on its own within the County of Gloucestershire the village and surrounding countryside became a type of "haven" for brigands during the seventeenth and eighteenth centuries. Those three flippantly referred to rogues Tom, Dick and Harry are amongst the most infamous characters of this period. All were members of the Dunsden family of Swinbrook and all three "operated out of Icomb". Reputed to have stolen £500 from the Gloucester mail they apparently boasted of their exploits in the local forest inns. As a result during a later exploit Dick Dunsden lost an arm and was never seen again but Tom and Harry were captured and went to the gallows in Gloucester in 1785, later to be left in chains on the famous Gibbet Oak in Swinbrook Parish.

Nowadays Icomb is a cosy little village of traditional Cotswold cottages set close together and enclosed by hills, woods and fine farmland. A village with a cross set in a small green where the main street opens out into a triangle.

Sir John Blaket who fought with Henry V at Agincourt was buried in the village church in 1431 leaving three shillings and four pence to the mother church at Worcester for the upkeep of his tomb. There is a local legend that a secret passage runs from beneath his tomb to Icomb House, the village's main house although no evidence of this has yet been found.

The Church of St Mary the Virgin has a most attractive porch which dates from the mid 1200s but the pride of St Mary's is the

Chancel which it is claimed is amongst the finest in the country and a perfect example of English architecture of the thirteenth century. The local residents are proud also of their collection of kneelers, all hand embroidered portraying all manner of country scenes, animal and bird life and numbering about thirty in all. If you are interested, pop in as you go by, but make sure your boots are clean.

St Leonard's at Bledington

31

4: *The Slaughters*

Map Landranger:	163
Start:	GR: SP 155 232
Distance:	3¹/₂ miles

The very popular and attractive villages of Upper and Lower Slaughter are linked by this short, pleasant walk, part of which follows the course of the River Eye. Shortly after the start of the walk there is a section of a few hundred yards of very muddy track; the remainder of the route is over firm ground.

Route

1. At Upper Slaughter park in the car park at the intersection of three roads, near to the pathway to the church. With the church (left) and the large tree behind you walk down the road towards the ford. Just before reaching the ford, at another large tree, turn left and follow the right of way indicated by an arrow.

Upper Slaughter. The view from the ford with the right of way to the left of the river

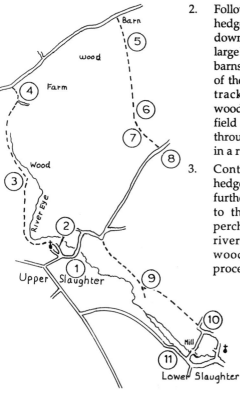

2. Follow the track, with a high hedge (left) and the river down to the right with the large Elizabethan house and barns on the opposite bank of the river. At the end of track pass through a wooden gate into an open field and follow the path through the next gateway in a ruined wall.

3. Continue ahead with a hedge on the right, soon a further gateway is visible to the left of a cottage perched high above the river. Pass through the wooden gateway and proceed down the track through the trees with the river below (right).

4. Pass Swiss Farm (right) and bear round left to the road ahead. At the road turn right and walk up the hill. As you round a bend at the top of the hill look out for a large barn now converted into a private residence on the right, to the right of which is a gateway with an arrow indicating the right of way. Pass through two gates into the field.

5. Keep to the left of the field close to a wire fence and later a wall. The field eventually slopes down a hill. Ahead is a wooden gate set in a stone wall with an arrow marker on the left pillar.

6. Go through the gate and turn sharp right as indicated. Keeping the wall on the right continue round the field passing a gateway at the top right corner.

7.   Pass a telegraph pole right and immediately turn right into another field. Turn sharp left and walk, with the wall and trees left, to the road.

8.   Across the road is Copse Hill Court. Turn right and go down the hill. At the bottom of the hill pass the side road to Lower Slaughter where the road bends right, turn left through a metal gateway in the wall and into a field. Pass through a further gateway in the fence ahead where the arrow indicates the right of way.

9.   Cross the next field and exit into a further field where the right of way is indicated by two arrows, at the metal gate. Follow the left diagonal arrow

Lower Slaughter

Beside the River Eye at Lower Slaughter

until you reach a further arrow at the entrance to the Cotswold Stud. Follow the right of way towards Lower Slaughter.

10. At the end of the track exit via the double gate onto the road and continue ahead with West Allotment Cottage (left). Take the first right, down the street of modern houses then past the post office and Mill (right) into the main street of Lower Slaughter.

11. Join the road across the stone foot bridge and with the water mill across the river (right) walk up the road with the river right. Continue along the road to the T-junction. Turn right and enter Upper Slaughter again.

Places and Points of Interest Along the Way

THE SLAUGHTERS

The name Slaughter comes from the Saxon meaning "the place of pools" or "place of sloe trees" and is not thought to have been derived as the result of a killing or an ancient battle ground.

Both Upper and Lower Slaughter are enhanced by their close proximity to the River Eye which flows through both villages. The better known of the two is Lower Slaughter with many of its houses lining both banks of the river. The river is little more than a few inches deep as it runs between stone lined grassy banks and under a number of attractive stone and wooden bridges.

At the top of the village of Lower Slaughter stands a nineteenth-century brick built watermill looking somewhat out of place amidst the typical Cotswold stone houses. The Church of St Mary, largely re-built in 1867, blends in well with its surroundings

as does the seventeenth-century Manor House which is now a hotel.

Upper Slaughter is set in more undulating countryside than its neighbour but is equally attractive in its own way. The stone

The ford and old bridge at Upper Slaughter

*River and cottages at
Upper Slaughter*

The mill at Lower Slaughter

cottages are more irregularly laid out and the Church of St Peter is situated on a low hill above the ford which crosses the river. The church is of Norman origin but was rebuilt to a large extent during the Middle Ages and contains numerous tablets and monuments dating from the seventeenth century; the diarist the Rev Francis Edward Witts was the rector during the 1800's and upon his death a Chapel was erected by public subscription to house his tomb. The seventeenth-century parsonage became known as The Manor, and it is now the Lords of the Manor Hotel. Just south west of the church is Wagborough Bush, a Bronze Age burial mound while to the east of the church is a castle mound dating from a later period.

Upper Slaughter is one of those "Thankful" villages having lost none of its inhabitants who served in either World Wars; consequently it does not possess a war memorial.

5: Whittington, Brockhampton, Sevenhampton, Syreford

Map Landranger:	163
Start:	GR: SP 014 208
Distance:	6 miles

This walk follows a route of many contrasts, both of terrain and of architecture. Best made in dry weather, the walk contains a number of quite steep climbs together with a gentler interlude along the valley of the infant Colne river.

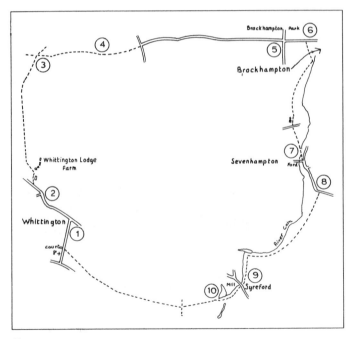

Cottages at Whittington

Route

1. Park in the village of Whittington. To commence the walk turn left at the T-junction signposted to Ham and go past the post box set into the cottage wall (right), then past the chapel (right).

2. At the sharp bend (left), continue straight ahead at the "No Through Road" sign walking along with a stream (left) until you reach Whittington Lodge Farm. Turn right into the track at the public right of way sign. At the farm buildings take the left fork, pass through a metal gate with a yellow arrow marker and climb up the hill. Continue to the top of the hill via a second gate followed by a gateway through a stone wall.

3. Walk straight ahead until a junction of tracks with blue and yellow arrow markers is reached and at the next wire fence go through a metal gate and turn right onto a footpath, walking by the wire fence (right). Soon a dip in the ground with hawthorn and other small trees is reached, the path marked by posts with an arrow marker curves slightly left; follow it round and walk with the trees on your right away from the wire fence.

41

The gatehouse to Brockhampton Hall

4. At the end of the trees pass a marker (right) and descend the hill passing two further markers (right), then crossing two stiles at the bottom of the hill, take the path straight ahead climbing up through the woods. Cross a further stile, go across the field, crossing a second stile and continuing ahead with a stone wall (left) until a track is reached. Turn left and immediately right following the track down the hill.

5. At the cross roads go straight ahead to the right of Brockhampton Lodge where a notice reads "Brockhampton Park Private No Entry", pass it (left) and just a little way further is a stile (right) with an arrow marker on it, just before the village of Brockhampton. If you wish to visit the village go straight ahead returning to the stile to continue the walk.

6. Cross the stile into the field to continue alongside a metal fence (left). The path follows the ridge with the river below left and goes across the fields emerging into the churchyard via a metal kissing gate. Walk through the churchyard, out across t' le lane ahead and through the wooden gate into the field aiming for the bottom left corner. Exit onto a path which takes you over the footbridge to cross the river.

7. Walk past the cottages with the river right, and at the ford turn left at Sevenhampton, then immediately right at the post box

set into the wall (right). Walk up the hill leaving the river below right. Eventually passing the last farmhouse with outbuildings left, pass through a metal gate onto a track, follow it up the hill until you reach the next metal gate.

8. Pass through the gate, turn right walking down the field with a stone wall on the right, passing a metal barn (left) and go through a further metal gate. Follow the path across the field to a wooden gate directly ahead, pass through it into a wood and continue until you exit onto a gravel track. Follow the track to the road.

9. Cross the road and continue ahead passing Old Syreford Mill with the river to the right. Shortly the track takes you into an attractive water garden where the public right of way, which is clearly marked, curves right and passes the rear of the private property.

10. Passing the lake (right), emerge at the arrow marker and cross the fields back to Whittington. The path is clearly marked by arrows. On reaching the

"Waste Not, Want Not",
is the inscription above
the crumbling old
water faucet at
Whittington

43

Whittington Court

road just opposite the entrance to Whittington Court, turn right to the village.

Places and Points of Interest Along the Way

WHITTINGTON

The tiny picturesque village of Whittington consists of little more than a couple of blocks of lovely old terraced cottages, a few larger houses, a couple of rather dilapidated barns, the manor house and a small church.

The Church of St Bartholomew's stands in the garden of the manor of Whittington Court. The manor, which is mentioned in the Domesday Book, is thought to have stood here since Saxon times. The church has indications of an early Norman origin and it is possible that the south aisle and the Norman arch were originally part of an older castle or fortified manor. The architecture of the church is unusual for this part of the England as it has a small wooden bell tower with a sharply pointed roof. Inside the church on the floor of the south aisle are three early fourteenth-century effigies, one of a lady and the others armoured knights. It is thought that these figures represent Richard de Crupes who died in 1278; his son, who like his father became lord of the Manor of Whittington, and the wife of one of the knights. Just outside the sanctuary rails is the monumental brass of Richard Cotton who built the mansion much as we see it today. Unfortunately for him he was killed in a duel a short time before the work was completed.

SEVENHAMPTON

A ford crosses the River Colne at Sevenhampton and the cottages are scattered along the river banks. The village church, with its Norman origins, is architecturally quite unique. The perpendicular central tower, added during the late fifteenth century is supported inside the church by flying buttresses and it also has vaulting under the belfry.

The ford, Sevenhampton, in winter   45

6: Salperton, Hazleton

Map Landranger:	163
Start:	GR: SP 076 203
Distance:	5¼ miles approx

This route combines track, road and occasionally cross-country walking in and around Salperton Park. This is high wold country and at every point the walker is rewarded with magnificent views across the high rolling countryside of fields and copses mingled with fine farm architecture.

Route

1. At Salperton park the car near the telephone box. With the telephone box left walk along the road to the large memorial (left) at the road junction. Turn left and climb the hill until the cross roads is reached, with Salperton Park House (left).

2. Turn right, follow the track through the woods for about

The memorial to James Harter of Salperton Park House

½ mile until the road is reached at Penn Hill. Turn left, walk about ½ mile along the road until the road forks. Take the left fork signposted Hazleton and continue for about ¾ mile until the T-junction is reached.

3. Turn left, left again and left again, into the village and follow the road down to the church. At the T-junction turn right, pass the church (right) and proceed until you pass the last bungalow on the left. Here the tarmac surface gives way to a track turning left and descending the hill, with

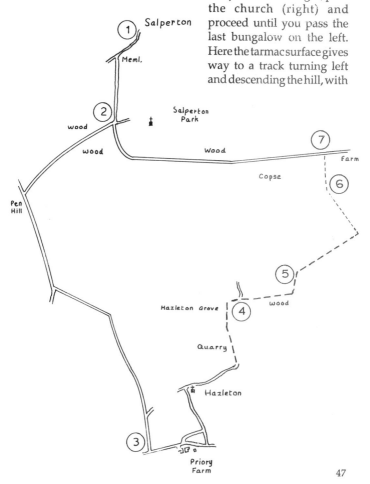

47

Hazleton Grove to the left.

4.   Where the track turns uphill to the farm there is a single gateway straight ahead, go through it. The right of way continues with the fence and a copse right and steep hills left. At the end of the copse is a wall with fencing at right angles to the right of way, turn left and climb the hill with the wall right.

The church at Hazleton

Farm buildings and the Glebe at Hazleton

5.   When you reach a gateway go through it and continue up the field diagonally right to the top corner (right). Go to the top left corner of the next field to a single wooden gate.

6.   Go through the wooden gate, follow the right of way directly across the next field and through the gateway, straight ahead, with hedges (left) and fencing (right).

7.   At the road go left and follow the road past a small copse (left) then a large copse (right). The road curves around right passing the church and Salperton House (right). At the bottom of the hill turn right past the memorial and return to the telephone box.

Places and Points of Interest Along the Way

SALPERTON

The tiny village of Salperton seems quite lonely and isolated. The village itself is little more than a few cottages intermingled with a number of handsome old barns, many in the process of being converted into private dwellings. On the outskirts of the village is the nineteenth-century Salperton House with its fine park originating from the seventeenth century. The small church has a Norman chancel arch and a medieval wall painting of a skeleton carrying a spear.

Game birds abound in the woods around Salperton

Shortly after the start of the walk the route passes the tall, rather stark memorial to James Harter. The inscription tells that in 1917 he died, from wounds, near Jerusalem "while helping to free the Holy Land from the hand of the infidel". The inscription also mentions that one of his ancestors had fought in the crusades during the thirteenth century for the same reason.

HAZLETON

Hazleton is a little larger than Salperton and consists of a collection of houses, cottages and farm buildings many of which have now been converted to private houses. Prior to 1885 Hazleton was well known locally for having the largest barn in the country. Unfortunately it burnt down and the story goes that it was so big it took two weeks to burn.

In the village churchyard there is a coffin thought to be 800 years old.

7: Notgrove, Cold Aston, Turkdean

Map Landranger:	163
Start:	GR: SP 109 202
Distance:	7 miles

This is a fine walk amidst some of the most attractive small hamlets and villages in the high wolds. Notgrove, Cold Aston and Turkdean are linked together by footpaths and bridleways which traverse rich farming country, hillside and woodland and a pleasant place to stop on this circuit is the Plough at Cold Aston.

The Plough at Cold Aston

Route

1. At Notgrove park the car facing the telephone box. Turn left, walk up the hill away from the village and at the road junction go left indicated To The Church.

2. At the steep hairpin bend in the lane go through the wooden gate straight ahead of you with a row of cottages (right). (The Church entrance is via the wooden gate in front of the cottages.) The right of way goes straight down the dip in the field and climbs up the opposite bank leaving through the gate ahead.

3. Pass through the gate onto the track, turn right then left onto the bridleway between the trees. Continue along the bridleway for about $5/8$ mile and at the road turn right towards Cold Aston, a further $1/4$ mile. On entering the village pass the track (right) marked "Unsuitable for Motors" and bear right to the village centre.

4. Pass the Plough (right) and turn onto the pathway (right) just after the road forks. Walk down the pathway for $1/4$ mile until it joins a bridleway.

5. Turn left along the bridleway, through the fields for a further $1^1/4$ miles until Turkdean is reached. At the road turn left, follow round right and past the church left. At the left bend take the lane (right).

6. Take the next right footpath, continue for about $1/4$ mile and at the junction with a track, bear left and continue along this track. Follow round (left), with a stream (left), then bear right at the junction.

7. Continue ahead then bear left leaving the stream to climb the steep hill and to pass to the left of the barn ahead.

8. Pass through the metal gate, turn left and with the stone wall on the left walk up the field, then follow the path diagonally right to the bridleway aiming for the copse of trees in the distance.

9. Turn right on the bridleway passing through the metal gates until eventually joining a concrete track close to the farm buildings ahead.

10. At the road turn left, then right to return to Notgrove.

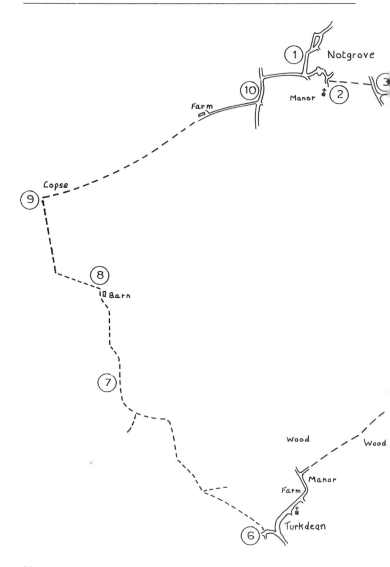

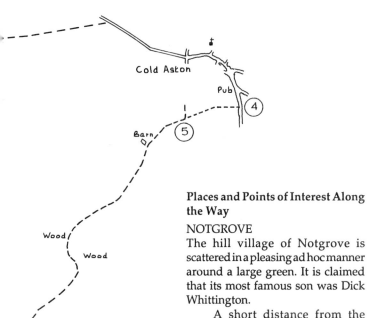

Cold Aston

Pub

(4)

(5)

Barn

Wood

Wood

Places and Points of Interest Along the Way

NOTGROVE

The hill village of Notgrove is scattered in a pleasing ad hoc manner around a large green. It is claimed that its most famous son was Dick Whittington.

A short distance from the village itself, a fine tree lined drive leads to the manor and church. The Norman church was extensively renovated during the nineteenth century but there are three interesting sixteenth- to seventeenth-century effigies of some of Dick Whittington's descendants to be seen in the chancel.

About a mile west of the village is a long barrow of 150ft length. The contents, remains of nine persons, are now housed in the Cheltenham museum.

COLD ASTON or ASTON BLANK

High up in the wolds, surrounded by beautiful views, sits the village originally called Aston. Around 1255 it became known as Cold Aston only to be changed again in 1535 to Aston Blank. The

Drystone walling at Notgrove

isolated and exposed position of the village is mirrored in the solid architecture of its houses.

TURKDEAN

Turkdean is a small hamlet set in the high wolds. It consists of a small collection of houses and cottages together with the Norman church of All Saints which was extensively renovated in the fifteenth century.

The hill village of Notgrove is scattered around a large village green

8: *Fifield, Idbury, Bruern Abbey*

Map Landranger:	163
Start:	GR: SP 239 187
Distance:	5 miles

This walk, across the rolling countryside links the small pleasant villages of Fifield and Idbury. Around Bruern Abbey the woodlands and fast flowing streams offer an attractive change of scene. In wet weather parts of the route can become quite muddy.

Route

1. Park outside the church at Fifield. Walk down the road, with the church left. Follow round (left) passing the metal barns (right) and continue until you reach Brambles Farm (right), where the right of way is on the left of the entrance.

2. Go through the metal kissing gate with the yellow arrow marker and leave via a second metal kissing gate into a field. Walking along the left side of the field with a wire fence (left). Cross the stile straight ahead, walk down the field, cross a further stile in a hedge at the bottom of the field, cross the bridge over the stream and pass through the gate. Walk up the field and continue ahead across a footbridge over a second stream. Aim

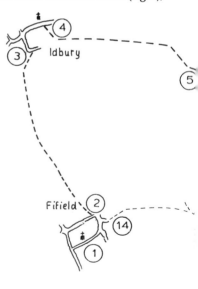

slightly diagonally right towards a large tree where a "step-over" stile is just to its right.

3. Once over the stile walk ahead close to the hedge (left). In the next field the right of way curves right to the stile which can be seen ahead at the edge of the village. Cross the stile, turn left and follow the lane until the road is reached at Idbury. Go right and pass the church left, then take the bridleway which is clearly marked (right).

4. Pass through two gates, then a third gateway and turn left onto

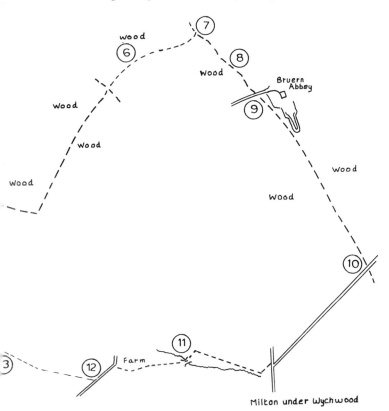

*A rather grand, old gateway towards
the bottom of Church Street, Fifield*

a track. With the woods directly ahead follow the track through the field. As the track passes through a hedge close to the wood, the bridleway is indicated right; follow it diagonally across the field to the top (right).

5.   At the top right pass between the hedges via the gate, turn left and walk ahead close by the wood (left). At the end of the wood turn left along a track and where the tracks cross continue ahead through a clearing with a wire fence (right).

6.   Walk past the Foxhole Nature Reserve (left), eventually leave the woods and go into a field and walk along the field with the woods close by (left).

7.   Where the woods end turn sharp left then immediately right onto a track. Ahead is a gate with a stile and a yellow arrow marker. Go over the stile and walk down the field by a wire fence (right). At the bottom of the field cross the track by way of two stiles, enter the next field and with woods on the right beyond the wire fence walk on until the exit with the yellow markers is reached.

8.   Cross the stile onto a path, go right, soon emerging from the

Cross the stile and walk up the lane into Idbury

woods into a field. With the woods on the right, walk ahead until the road is reached.

9. Cross the road and follow the markers of the Oxfordshire Way past Bruern Abbey (left), then across the field with a bank of trees ahead. Continue through a further two gates with markers and at the second enter a field and by a hedge (right) walk to the road.

10. At the road go right, follow it to Milton Under Wychwood. At the T-junction cross the road and go through the gate into the allotments. Turn left, proceed past the rear of the houses then follow the track by the river (left) until the footbridge is reached at the left corner.

11. Cross the bridge into the field and aim towards the left of Grange Farm, diagonally ahead. Pass to the left of the buildings, then bear right onto a track towards the metal gate with the right of way sign. Pass through the gate onto the road. Turn left and walk up the road passing farm buildings and houses (right). Enter the field (right) at the bridleway sign indicating Fifield 1 mile.

12. Walk diagonally across the field aiming just left of the bank of trees. Go through the gate with the yellow arrow marker into the next field, turn right and walk by the hedge (right). To the left of the right-hand corner is a stile in the hedge,

Bruern Abbey

cross it and then a footbridge into the next field.

13. With the stream (right) walk straight ahead, pass through the metal gate directly ahead and, following the line of the three telegraph poles, walk up the field to the stile in the hedge ahead of you. Cross the stile, turn left into the village recreation ground and join the road past a row of cottages (left).

14. Turn left on the road, then immediately right and walk up the street to the church.

Places and Points of Interest Along the Way

FIFIELD

Fifield is an attractive little village full of cottages and farm buildings.

The Church of St John the Baptist, Fifield

In the Domesday Book Fifield was described as having five hides, a hide being an area of approximately 600 acres of land. The village at this time was

63

therefore called Fifhide and over the centuries it has become Fifield. It was held by Henry de Feriers, a Norman knight, on behalf of William the Conqueror. The Church of St John the Baptist was founded about 150 years after the Domesday recording. The church has a unique octagonal spire which rises from a fourteenth-century octagonal tower. The church's communion chalice dates from 1546 and is still in use today.

The car park at Charlbury railway station is an exellent place to park. (Walk 9)

9: Charlbury, Wychwood Forest, Finstock, Cornbury Park

Map Landranger:	164
Start:	GR: SP 353 194
Distance:	6½ miles

This walk is essentially one for those who enjoy the forest with its ever changing colours throughout the various seasons.

After the steady climb from Charlbury we continue for about 2 miles through Wychwood Forest to the village of Finstock and return through farmland and amidst the woodland again of Cornbury Park.

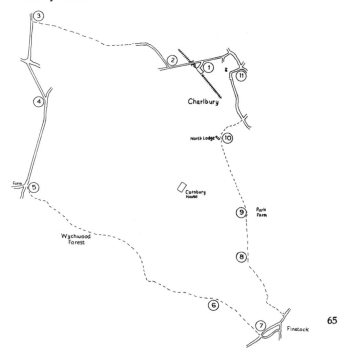

The pathway is clearly marked in the forest and in the park, and when not surrounded by woodland the splendid views across miles of rolling countryside can be enjoyed at all other times on this walk. We use side road, path and track and with a steady climb for the first half and a steady descent for the second half of the route the going is not strenuous.

Route

1. At the weekend park your car at Charlbury Railway Station. Mid-week it is best to park at the Spendlove Centre in Charlbury. Walk out of the railway station car park, turn left, cross the road and walk up the road crossing the railway line, continuing until you reach the sign marked Walcot Only.

2. Turn right through the gateway and walk down the track until you pass the cottages (right), continue ahead onto the Bridleway To Chilson, which is now part of the Oxfordshire Way. Pass the ruined barn (right) and continue ahead until you reach the road via a metal gate.

3. Turn left and begin the steady climb up to the cross roads where you should go straight ahead towards Leafield and continue walking up between the trees.

4. At the next road junction continue in the direction of Leafield for about $5/8$ of a mile where a track (right) leads to farm buildings, turn left and cross the stile where yellow arrow markers indicate the public right of way and the sign reads Finstock 2 miles.

5. Take the left fork indicated by the yellow arrow marker and follow the clearly indicated path through Wychwood Forest. Follow the yellow arrow markers for the next 2 miles and do not stray from the right of way.

6. After crossing a wooden stile the route crosses open farmland just before passing between old cottages as you arrive at the main road at Finstock. To visit the village cross the main road and follow the street round (left) or continue along our route.

7. Turn left, walk down the road, pass the Crown Hotel (right), shortly cross the stone stile (left) into a field and walk right of

a ruined barn where a yellow arrow marker indicates the right of way. Walk ahead down the track, noting the beautiful views across to the right, follow the track round, with fence and stone wall on the right, until you reach a large clearing at the junction of four tracks.

8. Where the wide, grassy tracks converge, go straight ahead following the arrow markers, descending gradually with fences

Leave Wychwood forest between the old cottages at Finstock

on both sides. Up on the hill amongst the trees (left) can be seen Cornbury House. At the end of this straight stretch of track the right of way marker is clearly visible to the left of the fence in front of you. Leave onto a narrower pathway with

The narrow streets of Charlbury

fences both sides and follow the path round onto a track at Park Farm.

9.   Turn left onto the track and walk over the causeway at the head of the lake. Go through the gate to the right of the cattle grid at South Hill Lodge marked "Footpath" and follow the yellow arrow marker. Walk along the path by the Deer Park (left) and leave via the garden of the gatehouse through the wooden door onto the roadway at Cornbury Park North Lodge.

10. Turn right, follow the road round crossing the river, then the railway and at the road junction turn left. Walk to Charlbury where you should turn right up Church Street passing the Bell Hotel (right).

11. At the top of the hill turn left, pass the post office (right) and left again at the sign post to the B.R. Station, down Dyers Hill from where the wooden station buildings can easily be recognised.

Places and Points of Interest Along the Way

CHARLBURY

The town of "free men" as it was called originally dates back to Saxon times. At the time of Domesday the Manor of Charlbury belonged to the Bishop of Lincoln, however in 1094 it passed to

Eynsham Abbey. During the seventeenth century Charlbury made its money from making gloves, though within the following 200 years the economy came to depend on agriculture.

The vast majority of the buildings in Charlbury date from the seventeenth century. However, some even older buildings can be found: in Thames Street Armada Cottage and the Old Talbot date back to 1587, whilst the Priory dates, in part, from the Middle Ages although it was mostly constructed during the Tudor and Stuart periods.

In 1870 the Old Market House which was situated at the top of Church Street was demolished. About 23 years earlier it had been the scene of a wife selling. The woman, who had a halter around her neck, was apparently sold for 2/6d after which her new owner, her former husband and the wife retired to The Bull and drank the proceeds of the sale. Bull baiting was still carried out at Charlbury until 1820 as was badger baiting, the latter being the sport of the grooms attached to the Heythrop Hunt.

The Bell Inn, Charlbury

The interior of the church at Charlbury, St Mary's, was described by Pevsner as having a "bleak and purged appearance after extensive restoration". This was probably due to the fact that the fortunes of Charlbury over the centuries were fairly humble when compared to some of its neighbouring towns and villages to the west, this meant that there would have been a shortage of wealthy patrons and benefactors to give to the church. The church is actually not much different in design or workmanship from most other local churches, it has some evidence of Norman work but in the main it was constructed during the thirteenth and fourteenth centuries. Legend has it, however, that St Diuma, first Bishop of the Mercians who died in 658, was buried here.

WYCHWOOD FOREST and CORNBURY PARK to CHARLBURY

Today Wychwood Forest forms part of the Cornbury Park estate. It is owned by Lord Rotherwick and 647 acres of it have been designated by the Nature Conservancy Council as a national nature reserve. The forest is home to a huge variety of trees: ash, elm, oak, sycamore and beech, to name but a few.

At one time in the past it seems that the Earl of Leicester had considered putting a fence around "all Wychwood, to keep in the deer and the people out", apparently the people of Charlbury were known to invade the forest in days gone by.

FINSTOCK

At Finstock the villagers were deprived of a Lord of the Manor, the absentee landlords of Charlbury Manor being Evesham Abbey and later St John's College, Oxford.

Until 1842, when the Duke of Marlborough gave land for the building of a chapel, the village had no church at all. Today's church, with its aisles, nave and chancel of 1905, is of little outstanding interest to the visitor except perhaps for the fact that Jane Baroness Churchill, who was maid to Queen Victoria for forty-six years, was buried here in 1900.

The Manor House at Finstock dates from 1660 and still is essentially Elizabethan, although some more recent additions have been made.

10: Little Rissington, Wyck Rissington, Bourton-on-the-Water, Great Rissington

Map Landranger:	163
Start:	GR: SU 191 200
Distance:	8$\frac{1}{2}$ miles

In my opinion this route includes all the good points of an enjoyable Cotswold walk: picturesque architecture, rivers, lakes and hills. Best undertaken in good weather, you will find that on a summer's day the area around the lakes, originally old gravel pits and now a water wildlife area, provides a peaceful contrast to the hurly-burly of nearby Bourton-on-the-Water.

Little Rissington

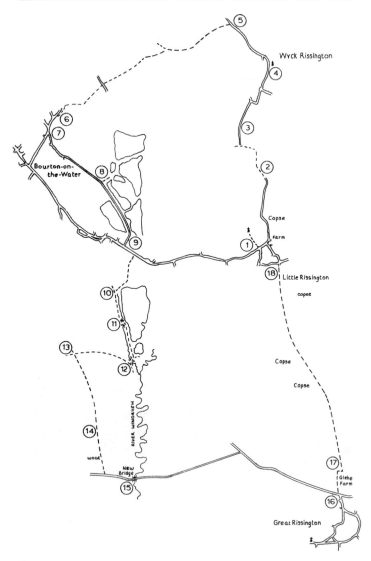

Route

1. Park in the Church car park, just beside the main road at Little Rissington. Turn left, walk past the row of cottages to the telephone box on the left. Walk along the bridleway (left) passing various barns until the track ends at a metal gate.

2. Cross the field down the hill bearing left. There are two gates in the opposite hedge, pass through the left gate, turn sharply left then right and walk ahead with a line of trees (right). Pass through a gate straight ahead.

3. Follow the track until you arrive at Wyck Rissington.

4. Pass the church (right) and with the old water fountain and duck pond on the right, cross the green.

5. Join the Oxfordshire Way (left), where the post box faces it across the road. Continue along this track until eventually you pass through a metal kissing gate. Ignore the Oxfordshire Way sign (right). Continue straight ahead through the field with a hedge (right).

The old water source at Wyck Rissington

6. Follow the arrows to enter Bourton-in-the-Water behind a housing estate by way of a stile onto a track. This in turn leads into Roman Way. To visit the town walk straight ahead, return to this point to continue the walk.

7. Take the next left turn up a track marked "Unsuitable for Motors", passing the graveyard and later the allotments. Continue down the track until the Cotswold Carp Farm (right) is reached.

The river at Bourton-on-the-Water

8. Take the stile (right) and follow the right of way behind the housing estate passing between two lakes eventually emerging onto a track. Bearing right over a further stile, continue down the track to the road.

9. Turn left and continue for a few hundred yards until you see the right of way sign across the road on the right. Follow the right of way for a short distance, then where the arrows indicate, cross the stile and ahead you will see a lake.

10. At the lake the track turns left. Continue along the path passing through woodland before emerging into a field. Cross a further stile and bear left over the next stile.

11. Following the path, cross a footbridge and continue to the end of the lake.

12. Turn right, pass through a couple of gates and cross the river by a wooden bridge. Continue over a stile into a field and at the marker bear right. Cross this small field and climb over another stile into the next field. Continue ahead, skirting the field, until a large gate with a marker comes into view.

13. Go over the stile and up the track until the tracks join. Follow the markers to the left; ahead are some farm buildings.

14. Go though the gate right of the farm buildings and continue along the right of way. Pass through a gate onto the road. Turn left and walk towards New Bridge.

15. Cross the bridge, continue along the road to the T-junction, turn right and walk up the hill towards Great Rissington, a further 1¹/₂ miles.

16. At the next road junction turn right to visit the village; to continue the walk turn left before the farm. Follow the bridlepath through the farm.

17. Pass through two metal gates, at the second turn sharp right, then left through a wooden gate and by a high hedge (left) walk along the left side of the field, following the markers, along the track in the direction of Little Rissington.

18. At the end of the track turn left into Pound Lane, continue down right until the church is reached.

Places and Points of Interest Along the Way

BOURTON-ON-THE-WATER

The immensely popular town of Bourton-on-the-Water is set along the broad banks of the shallow River Windrush where the streams flow in from the high wolds and journey on to the Thames Valley.

The history of Bourton goes back to Roman times when the Fosseway, the Roman road, was supported by a bridge across the Windrush. Also evidence of an Iron age hillfort has been excavated at nearby Salmonsbury. Little remains of the former town until one moves away from the main street to where examples of the unspoilt architecture of yesteryear can still be seen in patches. The Church of St Lawrence was built by the Normans on Saxon foundations, but the earliest remains visible today are the chancel dated from 1328 and built over a crypt of 1120, the uniquely domed tower dated from 1784 and the porch and nave from the 1800s. With its many additions during different periods of architecture St Lawrence's no longer looks the typical Cotswold church that one expects.

Today the town has developed to suit the tourist trade and on a fine summer day, tour buses jockey for position and the town becomes a mass of visitors. Amongst the many attractions to encourage the tourist to part with his cash is the Motor Museum which is housed in an old mill near the town centre, a model railway museum in the High Street, a model village, a butterfly exhibition, the Perfumery where visitors can sample and watch the blending of various perfumes and Birdland. Added to this is a collection of snack bars, fish and chip shops, restaurants, coffee shops and numerous hotels to suit all wallets.

THE RISSINGTONS

It is not unusual in England to find villages named in pairs and pre-fixed by Upper, Lower, Great or Little, but with the Rissingtons this practice extends to three villages - Little Rissington, Great Rissington and Wyck Rissington.

At the time of the Domesday Survey in 1086 Little Rissington consisted of 22 households. It is thought that the village was greatly affected by the Black Death in 1349 but only 32 years after this date the poll tax assessment indicated that the village had 44 tax paying adults. Today Little Rissington's main street is a collection of

The church at Wyck Rissington

seventeenth- and eighteenth-century Cotswold stone houses closely following the main road as it climbs out of Bourton-on-the-Water and curves through the village. Little Rissington's Church of St Peter has suffered considerably from nineteenth-century restoration, but the buildings oldest feature, the arcade of two twelfth-century Romanesque arches, is still intact. The church retains a strong connection with the now almost disused RAF base a mile or so away, for in the churchyard are buried no less than 75 men who died whilst serving in the RAF. Of these, 46 died during the Second World War and the west window is dedicated to their memory.

At 17 years of age Gustav Holst, who lived in a cottage close by, had his first professional engagement as organist of the Church of St Lawrence at Wyck Rissington. Architecturally the church is considered to be quite special with the base of the tower measuring nine feet thick thus suggesting that it could be even earlier than twelfth century, while the chancel and unusual trefoil pierced battlements a-top the tower are probably thirteenth century.

In 1950 Canon Harry Cheales who was the church rector had a dream in which he found himself to be looking out from a window of the rectory onto the garden at the centre of which was the sequoia, the big tree planted by a former Rector about a 100 years earlier. He was given direction in his dream on how a maze was to be constructed with the sequoia at its centre. The maze was opened on Coronation Day 1953 but on the Canon's retirement in 1980 it was taken apart and the rectory sold. The maze has always been regarded as a spiritual pilgrimage, wrong turns being life's pathways and the centre being heaven, so when the Rector died a memorial to him in the form of his maze created in Italian marble was placed in the north wall of the nave.

Overlooking the Windrush and its attendant water meadows is Great Rissington where the main street climbs a steep 200ft through the clusters of typical Cotswold dwellings. Here the Church of St John the Baptist is of Norman origin. The oldest parts are the four central pillars and arches which date from about AD 1200 and the porch is sixteenth century. Outside in the churchyard are three sepulchral slabs which are believed to be the graves of Crusaders.

11: Woodstock, Blenheim Palace

Map Landranger:	164
Start:	GR: SP 447 167
Distance:	7 miles

Although this walk starts and finishes in the pleasant town of Woodstock it is mainly through glorious parkland and offers spectacular views of Blenheim Palace and the 134ft high Column of Victory. Over gently undulating countryside the surface is mainly gravel or tarmac apart from one stretch along Akeman Street - the old Roman Road. The village inn at Combe makes an agreeable stopping place.

The village green, Combe, Oxfordshire

Route

1. At Woodstock the car park is between the fire station and the library/tourist information centre at Hensington Road. Leave the car park, turn right, walk down Hensington Road to the traffic lights. Cross the main road and bear right, down High Street, past the Crown Inn and Crown Cottage. Just after passing the Bear Hotel (left), with the town stocks (right), the road becomes Park Street.

2. Continue along Park Street and turn right into Chaucers Lane. At Harrison Lane (right) continue ahead down the steps of Hoggrove Hill and at the bottom turn left onto the main A34 road. Keeping on the left of the road cross the Causeway into Old Woodstock.

3. Pass The Black Prince (right), the Blenheim Orange Apple cottage (left) and continue up the hill to the footpath indicated left at the driveway between the cottages. Pass through the gate into Blenheim Park and follow the footpath ahead to the roadway.

4. Turn right, walk past the cottage (left) and follow the roadway as it takes you away from Queen Pool and climbs up and around between the

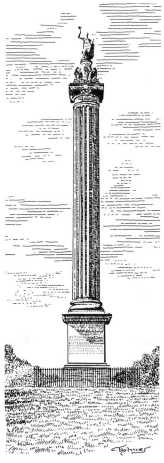

The Column of Victory,
Blenheim Park

81

trees, eventually bringing you to a right turn onto a long straight stretch.

5. After about ¾ mile the old Roman Road, Akeman Street, crosses at right angles and in the distance (right) are farm buildings known as Furze Platt. Turn left and by the fence (right) walk along the rough surface of Akeman Street through fields and after passing through trees,

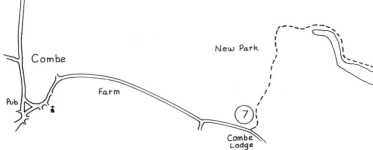

82

climb a ladder stile over a stone wall. Continue by the wall (left), crossing the field until the road ahead is reached.

6. At the road turn left, walk past Akeman Street Farm (right), walk up the hill into the village of Combe and continue straight ahead to the green which is overlooked by the village inn. Follow the road around (left), passing the church and the old post office (right) to walk out of the village. At the junction (right) continue ahead until you reach Combe Lodge.

7. Re-enter the park turning left along the roadway. Follow it through the trees and after the descent (right), with views of magnificent copper beech trees ahead, take the footpath off to the right. Walk by the fence (left), cross the stile, then follow the surfaced path (right) and continue with the lake on the right until you reach the junction of the roadway with the Grand Bridge.

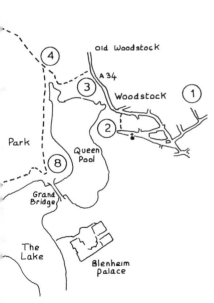

8. Turn right, then left to join the right fork of the roadway from the bridge. Follow the roadway with Queen Pool on the right until the junction is reached at the cottage. Go right, then left onto the footpath and leave Blenheim Park the same way as you entered from the main A34 road. At the road turn right and retrace your steps back to the car park.

Places and Points of Interest Along the Way

WOODSTOCK

The original manor house of Woodstock, home of the Black Prince, stood close to where the bridge is now situated in Blenheim Park. The house was damaged during the Civil War

Blenheim Palace

The Bear Hotel with the tower of St Mary Magdalene behind, at Woodstock

by the Cromwellians and then completely demolished in 1720 on the instruction of Sarah, Duchess of Marlborough.

The small town of Woodstock is a pleasant mixture of architectural styles from differing periods of history, straddling the road from Oxford to Stratford-upon-Avon. Solid stone buildings, such as Fletcher House, now the museum, and Chaucer's House, public houses and hotels such as the Marlborough Arms, and the Bear and Feathers, mingle well together with the Church of St Mary Magdalene and a variety of small shops to give a mixture of sophistication and attractiveness.

In the past glovemaking was widespread in Oxfordshire and today Woodstock is one of the few centres left. Woodstock gloves still adorn the hands of many distinguished persons.

On the other side of the River Glyme is the lesser known village of Upper Woodstock. As it is on our route it is worth mentioning an interesting point of agricultural interest. There is a plaque on the wall of one of the cottages as you climb the hill up from the river. It tells of the original Blenheim Orange apple being raised in the garden by George Kempsler, a tailor of Old Woodstock, who died in 1773.

BLENHEIM PALACE
Blenheim Palace, designed by Sir John Vanbrugh, was built for John Churchill, the first Duke of Marlborough, to demonstrate the nation's gratitude for his great victory over the French at Blenheim in 1704. One of the finest example of English Baroque and built of stone from Taynton (Walk 17) it houses a breathtaking collection of fine furniture, paintings, tapestries and sculpture. The library alone is a room of 183ft in length and houses over 10,000 volumes.

The Palace was the birthplace of Sir Winston Churchill and today the room in which he was born is open to the public. Also on show are a collection of his personal belongings, books, photographs, letters together with some of his paintings.

In the Palace grounds is the Marlborough Maze, the world's largest symbolic hedge maze opened to the public as recently as 1991. The lake, the home of many varied waterfowl and the 2,000 acres of parkland was Capability Brown's contribution to this fine estate during the late eighteenth century.

COMBE
Combe is set well above the River Evenlode which is joined beyond the village by the River Glyme as it flows out of the Great Lake at Blenheim. It is a typical Oxfordshire village with ancient cottages and houses, together with its old inn The Cock, spread around the edge of the large green.

Blenheim Park

12: Coberley, Leckhampton Hill

Map Landranger:	163
Start:	GR: SO 966 159
Distance:	5 miles

This is a fine walk from tiny Coberley with its unusual church surrounded by farm buildings, and its historical connections with Dick Whittington. It follows a well signposted, gradually ascending route over farmland, track and lane to the top of Leckhampton Hill with its stunning views. The return is by way of a gated road with runs along a pretty little valley.

Route

1. Park close to the farm buildings in front of the Coberley village church. With the church on the left, walk up the hill toward the

Coberley Post Office

village itself. Just before the post office turn right, passing the telephone box (right) walk by the front of the cottages where the notice (left) says "School - No Through Road".

2. Follow the lane round to the right, pass the school (left) and enter the bridleway ahead signposted Severn Springs 1km, Leckhampton Hill 3km. Walk ahead through the fields with a high hedge (right), eventually passing a stile (right) as the path curves left towards the A436 road ahead.

3. Cross the road, just to your left the path continues up steps, over a stile with a yellow arrow marker and with a

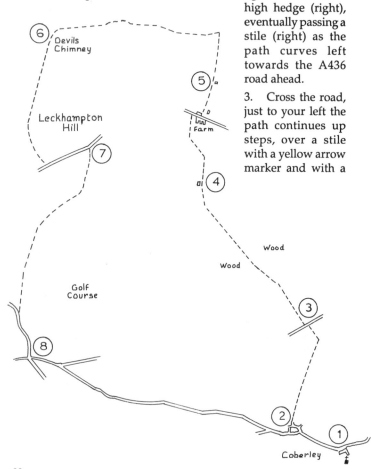

At Hartley Farm pass the metal barn, turn left and follow the sign to Leckhampton Hill

metal fence (right). Cross the next stile and with woods left and right, walk on until a further stile is reached, cross it and walk immediately right to a stile with an old brick building beyond it.

4. Climb over the stile, pass right of the building and walk up the hill by a copse (left), after which bear left and cross the stile (left) in the stone wall. Turn right passing the farm (right), and at the lane turn right. After the metal barn go left at the Leckhampton Hill 1 mile sign, walk up the track and cross a further stile with yellow arrow marker with ruined farm building beyond right.

5. With the wire fence on the right, walk ahead, cross the next stile, turn left and follow the well marked track with views of Cheltenham on the right, then through the trees until the flat plateau is reached atop Leckhampton Hill.

6. After admiring the views bear round left to follow the gently descending track until it narrows to a footpath with farmland

Cross the stile and pass the ruined farm building, right

(left) and a disused quarry below (right). At the roadway turn left, climb the hill until the Cotswold Way sign (right) is reached. Here take the right track signed Sherdington Hill.

7.   Follow the track down to the road junction, turn left, past the Cotswold Hill Golf Club club house and walk to the main A436 road ahead.

8.   At the road junction turn left in the direction of Oxford and

Down the gated road to Coberley

walk until the lane (right) is reached at the sign "Coberley 1 mile Gated Road", from where it is about 1¹/₄ miles to Coberley Church.

The Devil's Chimney on Leckhampton Hill

Places and Points of Interest Along the Way

COBERLEY

About a mile north of the tiny village of Coberley is Seven Springs, the place that vies with Coates as being the source of the River Thames. Seven Springs is so called because the water source consists of seven rather small and insignificant springs that run into a stream, this in turn becomes the River Churn which, it is argued, is in fact the Thames.

Coberley itself is merely a scattering of buildings with the Church of St Giles a short distance away down the hill. Barely visible from the roadway, the church is approached via the arched doorway of a large and handsome farm building. St Giles was rebuilt to a great extent during 1870 but the small porch and south chapel date from about 1340. The large effigies of knight and lady in the latter are generally accepted as being Sir Thomas Berkeley who fought at Crecy and his wife Lady Joan. They lived at nearby Coberley Hall which unfortunately was demolished during the eighteenth century. Following the death of her first husband in 1350, Lady Joan married a second time to Sir William Whittington, the father of "Dick", perhaps the most famous of pantomime characters and thrice Lord Mayor of London.

The entrance to the church at Coberley is through the arched doorway of the handsome old farm buildings

An unusual burial in Coberley's churchyard is that of Lombard, a favourite horse of another of the Berkeleys, Sir Giles Berkeley; but while his horse and his heart are buried here, he is not, he was buried at Little Malvern in 1295.

LECKHAMPTON HILL

Much of Cheltenham was built from the light creamy stone quarried at Leckhampton Hill. The Devil's Chimney, a tall single column of stone, is an existing monument to the extensive quarrying that was carried out on this 1,000ft high area over the centuries. At the summit of the hill are the remains of an ancient British hill fort, now a flat plateau with seats dotted about, the area is popular for its views over the surrounding countryside and Cheltenham.

The Giffards were a family of local renown many years ago in the Leckhampton area, in fact two of the sons were in their day members of a very prominent local gentry, a third son was a founder of Worcester College, Oxford but the fourth was hanged, his grand home being razed to the ground for attacking the king's baggage train near Birdlip.

13: *Sherborne Park, Sherborne, Windrush*

Map Landranger:	163
Start:	GR: SP 159 144
Distance:	5³/₄ miles

This walk starts at Sherborne Park, recently acquired by the National Trust, and follows a route down through the woods to Sherborne village. After passing through the village streets and along the banks of the Windrush to the Old Mill, the walker can divert to the village of Windrush before rejoining the walk to return along the opposite river bank to Sherborne village.

Route

1. Park in the National Trust car park at Sherborne Park. To start the walk follow the "medium" route through the park as indicated by the green arrows. On leaving the car park, turn right onto the track and walk to the end of the farm buildings. Turn slightly to the left as indicated by the green arrow and

Early spring at Windrush village

proceed along the edge of the field with the wire fence on your right. Follow the arrow markers all the way down through the woods until you reach the road.

2. Cross the road and turn right, pass the telephone box (right) and continue, passing the war memorial (right), past the post office (left), eventually reaching a road junction with a road sign indicating directions to Windrush and The Barringtons (right).

A ram's head corbel at
St Peter's church, Windrush

3. Turn left along the road until you are level with the last row of cottages (left), go right along a concrete track between cottages that soon gives way to a stile with right of way markers. Cross the stile, turn left and immediately right with a stone wall on your right. Follow the track around to cross the small stone bridge spanning the River Windrush.

4. Turn right and go diagonally cross the field aiming between the two sets of trees in the distance, crossing the stile and continuing straight ahead as indicated by the arrow marker leaving the woodland on the left.

5. Leave the field through the hedge with marker (left), turn right onto the right of way with the hedge on your right. Continue ahead until you reach the river at a blue arrow marker. Cross the river over the concrete bridge and follow the footpath ahead which soon turns left between the remains of some old buildings, eventually emerging from the woodland into farmland where the right of way turns to the right.

6. Follow the track (right) leaving the river behind you, going down to the right and to Manor Farm. After passing the recently restored main farm buildings, pass between a

magnificent old barn and a newer metal barn.

7. Leaving Manor Farm, follow the track straight ahead with a hedge on your left until you reach a metal gate in the hedge at the end of the field. Do not go through the gate but turn right keeping the hedge on your left. At the bottom of the field, cross the foot-

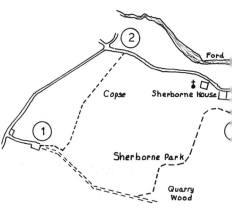

bridge, turn left into the field passing through the gateway into the adjoining field, aiming for the tower of Windrush Church that should be visible amongst the trees in the distance, walking towards the River Windrush once again.

8. At Windrush Mill turn right through the metal gate. Follow the track around to the left and between the mill buildings which is now a private residence. As you walk between the buildings, the right of way is to the left leading to a stone stile. Turn right to go up the field and over the stile straight ahead. (To visit the village of Windrush, continue straight ahead here and return to the route later).

9. To continue the walk, go right over the stone stile, cross the track to pass through the gate marked "To Sherborne". Follow the well indicated route back to the village. On reaching Sherborne, retrace your steps to the war memorial.

10. Across the road junction from the war memorial, there is a telephone box to the right of which is a gate. Go through the gate and follow the well defined track up through the woods, passing the ice house as you return to the car park along the farm track.

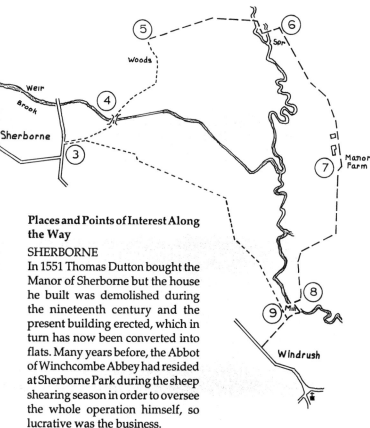

Places and Points of Interest Along the Way

SHERBORNE

In 1551 Thomas Dutton bought the Manor of Sherborne but the house he built was demolished during the nineteenth century and the present building erected, which in turn has now been converted into flats. Many years before, the Abbot of Winchcombe Abbey had resided at Sherborne Park during the sheep shearing season in order to oversee the whole operation himself, so lucrative was the business.

The Church of St Mary Magdalene has also been rebuilt, as was much of the east end of the village during the nineteenth century. The aim was to create a model village of the period, most of the cottages are therefore grouped in the form of terraced dwellings. Perhaps one the most attractive buildings in the village is the Victorian post office.

Recently the Sherborne estate has been acquired by the National Trust and work is being carried out on many of the old farm buildings, also a number of footpaths within the estate are being developed and very pleasant they are too. Our walk, taking in part of the estate, passes the old ice house, now cleared of undergrowth, and with a light on a time switch it is possible to see down into the depths of this Victorian brick lined cold store.

The River Windrush at Sherborne weir

WINDRUSH

This tiny but picturesque village is very readily acceptable to the visitor's eye, for nearly every building is a fine example of its type.

At the very edge of the River Windrush stands a seventeenth-century corn mill; at the village's centre is a small triangular green just in front of the Church of St Peter. The south doorway of the church is Norman with a double row of beakheads. The timbers of the nave rest on twelfth-century corbel heads and above the aisle arcade is a sheep's head corbel.

The old ice house, Sherborne Park

14: Northleach, Farmington

Map Landranger:	163
Start:	GR: SP 114 147
Distance:	4 miles

At the start of the walk there are fine views over the town of Northleach with the cathedral like tower of its church dominating the scene. Once on high ground the scene changes to distant woods and a rolling agricultural landscape. The route follows tracks and side roads with only a short distance on footpaths.

It would be advisable to allow time to visit the many points of interest in Northleach at the end of your walk.

Route

1. At Northleach, park in the car park near the post office. Start by walking along the High Street, past the Sherborne Hotel until you reach Dutton Lane, a narrow alley way (on your right) between the houses. Go down Dutton Lane, crossing the

Fine views over Northleach as the climb up to Helen's Ditch is made

The stile leaving Northleach

river and stile following the right of way markers. Walk up the hill bearing slightly right to the top of the hill, cross the stile and continue close to the wall (right) until you reach Helen's Ditch.

2. From Helen's Ditch, turn left and walk along the track with fine views down (left). At the road go right until you reach the footpath sign (left), cross three stiles onto the footpath and continue straight ahead through the field, keeping the stone wall on your left. Cross two more stiles and at the end of the stone wall, turn left through a metal gate and then over a wooden bridge

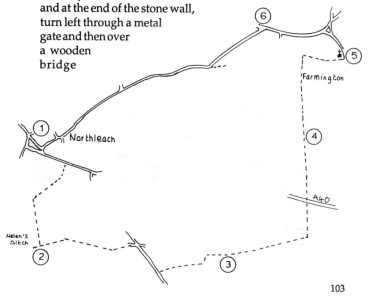

103

with a lake on your left.

3. Follow the track up the hill with the woods on the right, follow the signs across the fields, past a metal barn (left) and at the end of the next field, with a metal gate and two markers, turn left. Aim for the stile in the fence in the distance, cross the main road (A40), then continue along the field's edge, keeping the stone wall on your right.

4. Keeping to the right, continue along the right of way, through the fields, cross the river and climb the hill, go over a wire fence with no marker. The right of way now continues towards the Rectory in the distance. Before you reach the Rectory there is a metal fence, at the end of which, to the right, is a gateway in the stone wall. Go through this gateway, onto the track, turning left, then right passing the church (left) and join the road.

5. Turn left past the church and follow the road bearing left and past the village green to leave Farmington.

6. After passing the houses on your left, take the next left turn where there is a notice indicating a 7.5 tonne weight restriction, $1^3/_4$ miles ahead. Walk along this road to reach Northleach

Half-timbered and stone buildings at Northleach

where you cross at the end of the High Street, turn right into The Pete thereby returning to the car park.

Places and Points of Interest Along the Way

NORTHLEACH

Northleach derives its name from the fact that it was originally laid out on the north side of the River Leach. From around AD 800 the land around Northleach was owned by the Abbey of Gloucester and it was decided that the town be built in the shape of a "Y" with the market place at the fork. The town expanded considerably between 1340 and 1540 when the prime source of income was the export of wool to the continent. As the reputation of Cotswold wool grew so did the fortunes of the dealers known as the staplers. The merchants of the staple held a monopoly from the Crown and they alone had the Crown's authority to export wool. As a result of the

Northleach cartel John Taylor, William Midwinters, Thomas and John Fortey grew very rich. Later during the eighteenth and nineteenth centuries Northleach became a busy staging post between Gloucester and London.

The green at Farmington

Today Northleach is a most pleasant little town with a mixture of varying architecture centred around the market place and the area known as The Green. Facing the car park, which now occupies the green, the half-timbered house is said to have been the home of John Fortey whose badge is represented in the stone corbels of each side of the carriage entrance.

The Church of St Peter and St Paul, where sheep still graze amongst the gravestones, was largely rebuilt during the fifteenth century and it is regarded as one of the finest examples of the Cotswold wool churches. The south porch has crocketed pinnacles, medieval images and outside buttresses. Inside there is some fine vaulting and the corbels, especially the three rats listening as the cat plays the fiddle, should not be missed. John Fortey wished to make the church splendid and lightsome so he paid for the rebuilding of the nave and the addition of the clerestory. The evidence of the riches gained from the wool trade are in abundance and include many brasses of the wool merchants and their families.

A short stroll away from the centre of the town is the old mill situated at the edge of the River Leach. Nearby is the Cotswold Countryside collection, a museum of rural life housed in the eighteenth-century prison. The prison building was one of the earliest known "model prisons". Its designer Sir Onesiphorus Paul was a gentleman with a strong interest in the welfare was well as the correction of prisoners. These interests are reflected in the exercise yards, a sick bay, separate sleeping rooms and baths.

FARMINGTON

The village Church of St Peter's dating from Norman times has an interesting chevroned arch over its southern doorway and a chancel from the same period. The porch is from the fourteenth century. Other parts of this peaceful village are much younger in age; the Georgian mansion, Farmington Lodge, with its doric columns, has a circular dovecote and stables built in the eighteenth century. The octagonal Pumphouse, situated on the green, is late 1800s. The gentle sloping village green is particularly pleasant, being surrounded by old cottages and trees.

About half a mile away from the village, Norbury Camp is the site of a stronghold of the ancient Britons. To the south of this is a 150ft burial mound or Long Barrow.

15: Minster Lovell, Crawley

Map Landranger:	164
Start:	GR: SP 322 114
Distance:	2³/₄ miles

This short walk follows the River Windrush as it winds its way amidst the water meadows from Minster Lovell to Crawley. Both villages have pubs should you wish to use them and at Minster Lovell the lovely Church of St Kenelms is worth a visit as is the remains of Minister Lovell Hall.

Route

1. At Minster Lovell, park at the top of the road leading to the church. With the church on your right, walk along the road towards Crawley.

2. Soon after passing Manor Farm, cross right in to the field and walk diagonally away from the road towards the river. The footpath is fairly obvious as you cross the fields and the chimney of Crawley Mill dominates the distant skyline.

3. Eventually as you draw level with the mill across the river, join the roadway (left) near the first of a row of cottages. Turn right here and this will take you into Crawley.

4. At the road junction with the pub (left), turn right and walk down the road to cross the old bridge near Crawley Mill. Just after the bridge turn left onto the bridleway (right of way) following the river.

5. Walk along this path for about ³/₈ of a mile until you reach the junction of the tracks. Turn right here and go as far as the road where you cross over and follow the footpath through some trees with a river on the right.

6. As you leave the woods, the footpath across the

The Street, Minster Lovell

field is well defined with yellow markers.

7. On reaching the road, just in front of St Kenelms, turn left and this will return you to the starting point.

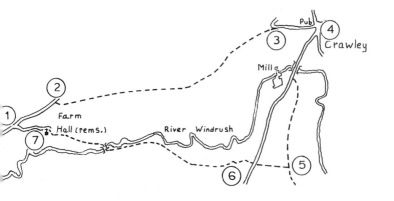

Places and Points of Interest Along the Way

MINSTER LOVELL

The main street of Minster Lovell is quite different from the villages further up the Windrush Valley. Being set further east into Oxfordshire the stone roofed cottages have changed, at least in part of the village, to thatch. An interesting point about these cottages is that at one time in their history the rent was sixpence (2$\frac{1}{2}$p) a year. Because the rent was so low it became uneconomical to collect so the occupants lived rent free. However, if a resident lived for a period of twelve years in the same cottage he had the right to own the building. In order to avoid this happening they were required to move all the contents out on to the street for a day during the

Minster Lovell, Oxfordshire

eleventh year.

The lovely old village church is dedicated to St Kenelm, the boy king whose sister saw to it in AD 822 that his life was only a short one. It was built partly on earlier foundations by the seventh Baron Lovell around 1431 and has been modified and refurbished over the years. It is an unusual design, a cruciform church with a central tower.

MINSTER LOVELL HALL

Amidst the grassy, willow-lined banks of the Windrush are the ancient, elegant and ghostly remains of the Minster Lovell Hall, now in the care of the Ministry of the Environment. Built in the

111

St Kenelm's Minster Lovell

fifteenth century by William, seventh Baron Lovell of Tichmarsh, they give an indication of life as it was centuries ago in this part of England.

At the Battle of Bosworth in 1485 the Viscount Lovell shared Richard III's defeat and promptly disappeared to France. After further defeats he fled back to Lovell Hall where a single servant hid him in a secret room. Two hundred years later what was thought to be his remains were found together with those of his dog; hence the reference to the ghostly remains of Minster Lovell Hall.

The ruins of Minster Lovell Hall

113

16: Burford, Fulbrook, Widford, Swinbrook, Asthall

Map Landranger:	163
Start:	GR: SP 255 123
Distance:	5³/₄ miles approx.

Leaving the busy town of Burford the route soon passes through the village of Fulbrook into the peaceful surroundings of the Windrush valley. The walk is mainly over flat terrain with only a couple of steady inclines but should you be weary with effort there are no less than four hostelries on route and that doesn't include the pubs and tea shops in Burford.

Route

1. Entering Burford from the North on the A424 or the A361, you will cross the narrow bridge over the River Windrush at the bottom of the High Street. The car park is a little way up on the left, just before the public toilets. From the car park, turn right and follow the road to the High Street. Turn right, walk down the hill and across the bridge. Turn right onto the A361 and walk up the hill into Fulbrook.

2. Turn right along the road to Swinbrook and as the road descends, and with a copse on your right, turn right immediately after a bridleway on your right, cross a stile with a yellow arrow.

3. The path descends between a long avenue of trees to Widford Church. Here you will cross a stile and join a track at a T-junction where you need to turn left and walk across fields, crossing cattle grids and stiles to Swinbrook.

4. On the outskirts of the village, pass through a gate in a stone wall and indicated by a yellow right of way marker. Follow this path between two stone walls, in front of a pair of cottages

Burford. The fourteenth-century almshouses near the church

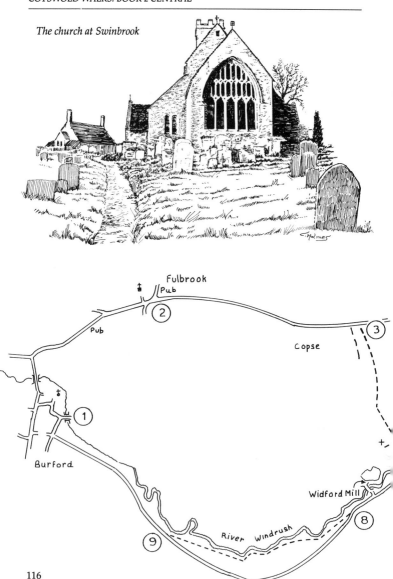

The church at Swinbrook

and subsequently the church. At the church, turn right onto the road that leads to The Swan public house.

5. Cross the road in front of The Swan, go over a stone stile and walk behind the cottage with the river on your right. Follow the arrow markers to the fence, cross the fields by way of stiles, bearing right towards the river, (Asthall Church and Manor are visible through the trees to the right) then bear left towards a stone wall.

6. Cross the stone wall via a stile and onto the road. Turn right to cross the bridge (note the carving of a musket in the stone on the right side of the bridge). Continue towards the village, turning right at the T-junction, then right again at the next junction to pass The Maytime Inn (right). Follow the road around to the left with the church on your right.

7. At the next T-junction, turn right and at the cross roads, go straight ahead and past the cricket ground eventually leading to Widford Mill.

8. Pass Widford Mill Farm on your right and just after cross the stile. Follow this path down to the river and walk along the bank, crossing three more stiles.

9. This last stile brings you onto the road. Turn right and into Burford, passing The Old Bell foundry (right), then the Great House (left). At Gildenford, turn right to return to the car park.

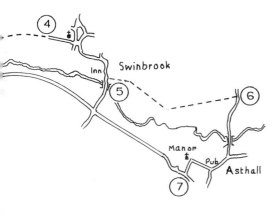

Places and Points of Interest Along the Way

BURFORD

One of my favourite Cotswold towns is Burford. The whole character and former prosperity of the Cotswolds is reflected in its medieval stone buildings erected with the profits of the wool trade. Long after the decline of this, the elegant, wide High Street and the surrounding side street became noisy with the clatter of horses hooves as Burford developed into a busy nineteenth-century staging town. At its peak around forty stagecoaches a day would clatter up and down the hill on the 24 hour long journey to London. Since that time the town's fortunes declined until the development of the family car spelt the growth of tourism and a new prosperity.

Back in 1175, there stood at Burford a simple church of Norman construction, but as the fortunes of the wool traders developed the Church of St John the Baptist was added to and "improved" over the following 300 years by which time it was very similar to the rather "irregular" church we see today. Indeed so much development went into the tower in the form of masonry plus 30 tonnes of bells, that the Norman arches of the tower had to be "built-in" in order to strengthen the structure. Henry VIII's surgeon, Edmund Harrison, is buried here as is the Lord Chief Baron of the Exchequer to James I, Sir Lawrence Tanfield. One of the master masons who built St Paul's Cathedral, Christopher Kempster, is also buried here.

The region as a whole saw much fighting during the English Civil War and Burford was not without its share of the action. In 1649, Cromwell had something of a rebellion on his hands and firm handling became necessary. More than 300 of his men were rounded up and imprisoned in the church, as an example three of them were shot in the churchyard. The event is commemorated by a plaque on the church's outer wall. One of the imprisoned soldiers scratched his name on the church font, if you look on the rim you can still make out "Anthony Sedley, Prisner 1649".

At right angles to the church, just by the green, are the lovely old almshouses built by the Earl of Warwick in 1457 and rebuilt in 1828. Just across from the almshouses is the sixteenth-century Boy's Grammar School.

There is much to interest the visitor in Burford, certainly the visitor with an interest in history. Priory Lane takes its name from the former sixteenth-century priory. It was bought by Sir Lawrence Tanfield and completely rebuilt but on his death the ownership passed to Speaker Lenthall of the Long Parliament, who had it enlarged and added a chapel. Little of the original building remains today though and it has now become the property of an enclosed order of nuns.

The Old Rectory, built in 1700, is in Priory Lane too and on the corner is Falkland Hall, which dates from 1558. On both

The heron is frequently seen along the River Windrush

sides of today's High Street are antique shops, hotels, tea shops, jewellers, newsagents and souvenir shops but many of these buildings have histories going back to the 1500s.

Up the hill, past Priory Lane, is the Wesleyan Chapel, built in the early eighteenth century and converted to a chapel in the late nineteenth century. The tolls for trading rights and for the fairs held at Burford were paid to the merchant's guild at the Tolsey, a fine medieval building at the corner of Sheep Street which now houses the museum. The first mention of the Tolsey is on a bill for a carpet dated 1561 when the building was known as the Court House, here the Burgess's Court met to settle disputes. At its rear was a prison known as a Blind House, the door of which is in the museum. In later years from about 1800 until 1956, the ground floor, which was enclosed, was used to house the town's fire tender.

Also in Sheep Street is the Bay Tree Hotel which was built during the reign of Elizabeth I by her Lord Chief of the Exchequer, the much disliked Sir Lawrence Tanfield. Evidence exists that Queen Elizabeth I visited Burford and it is almost certain that she would have stayed at the house of her most eminent politician. Further down the street is the fifteenth-century Lamb Inn which has functioned as an inn since the mid 1800s.

The best time to get the feel of Burford is in the early morning before it becomes clogged with traffic and busy with visitors. Walk to the top of the hill and admire the view down the High Street to where the Windrush flows beneath the narrow bridge and the church spire makes a sharp contrast with the fields and hedges that rise on the opposite bank.

At the bottom of High Street, just off the ancient bridge that spans the Windrush is the entrance to Ladyham, which means our Lady's field by the water. This beautiful old house, the home for centuries of the wool merchant family, the Sylvesters, was once owned by Sir Compton Mackenzie, the prolific author who was perhaps best known for *Whisky Galore*. He is said to have paid £1,400 for the house during the early 1900s; during 1992 it was for sale at £750,000.

FULBROOK
Fulbrook lies in close proximity to Burford with the River Windrush

forming a boundary between the two. The main point of interest about Fulbrook is its connection with Icomb (Walk 3) and Tom, Dick and Harry, for whilst they were reputed to have "operated" out of Icomb they came from Fulbrook. The gibbet oak is in a field just to the north of their native village.

WIDFORD

Standing isolated in a field that slopes up from the River Windrush is the tiny Church of St Oswald which was, at one time, surrounded by a medieval village. The church was constructed during the twelfth and thirteenth century, probably by the monks of Gloucester, on the former site of a Roman villa. One theory as to why the church was built here is that it may have been the site on which the body of St Oswald, a king of Mercia in AD 642, had rested on its journey from Lindisfarne to its burial at Gloucester. After 1859 the church was abandoned and was not restored until shortly after the turn of the century. The restoration revealed red and white Roman mosaics

The bridge over the Windrush at Widford Mill

St Oswold's church at Widford

The carving on the old bridge near Asthall

and fourteenth- and fifteenth-century wall paintings. The church also houses a thirteenth-century tub font and eighteenth- to nineteenth century boxed pews.

SWINBROOK

Swinbrook, like many other local villages has numerous tales of poachers and robbers who frequented the surrounding areas in years gone by. Today, however, this attractive village lives quietly beside the River Windrush. The Church of St Mary dates back to the twelfth century and was enlarged during the fifteenth century. The Fettiplace Monuments, however, are the real claim to fame here. They recline rigidly on one elbow, all six members of the same family, all from the seventeenth century. They are to be found on three shelves recessed into the north wall of the chancel. The Mitford sisters, Nancy and Unity, are buried in the churchyard.

ASTHALL

Asthall is a collection of roadside cottages, farms, a seventeenth century manor house and the lovely church of St Nicholas, all set in the water meadows of Oxfordshire. The village was originally a Roman settlement with Akeman Street, the Roman road, passing through it. Much later Esthale, as it was called in the Domesday Book was held for the King by Roger d'Ivery.

The Norman church stands on a slightly raised mound at the head of the main street, close to the manor house. A number of unusual features inside the church include Norman bird beaking around the chancel arches and faces of angels - both male and female - on the nave corbels. The north chapel was once a chantry chapel served from Burford Priory. It is divided from the chancel by a stone screen and its twelfth-century walls carry fourteenth-century decoration. On the north wall, below the window depicting the crucifixion, is an effigy underneath a decorated canopy. It is said to be of Lady Joan Cornwall, wife of Edmund, who was the grandson of King John. The church font dates from the early twelfth century.

Just behind the village a stone bridge crosses the river and on the western parapet appears a carving crudely representing a German rifle and helmet. This was carved by Bert Francer while he was recovering from his wounds in the temporary hospital, at the manor, during the First World War.

The church of St Nicholas, Asthall

17: Burford, Little Barrington, Great Barrington

Map Landranger:	163
Start:	GR: SP 254 124
Distance:	6¼ miles

This is a fine walk along the lanes and side roads of the Windrush valley. It is a good one to save for a time of year when the weather is past its best and the footpaths and bridleways are heavy and sticky with mud.

If you have entered Burford from the north on the A424 or on the A361 you will cross the narrow bridge over the River Windrush at the bottom of the High Street. The car park is signposted a little way up on the left, just before the public toilets.

The Lamb Inn, Burford

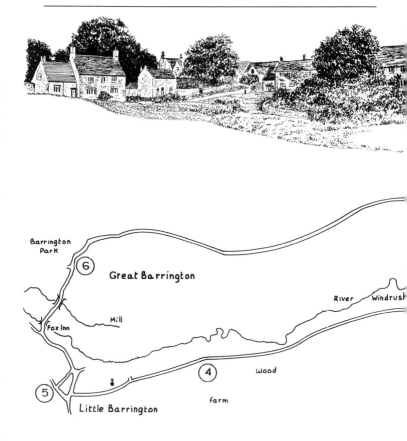

Route

1. Leave the car park in its picturesque setting beside the river and walk back to the main road passing the vicarage (left) and the church, the almshouses and the old school buildings (right). On reaching the High Street turn left, cross the road at the traffic lights and continue up the hill until you reach Sheep

The green at Little Barrington

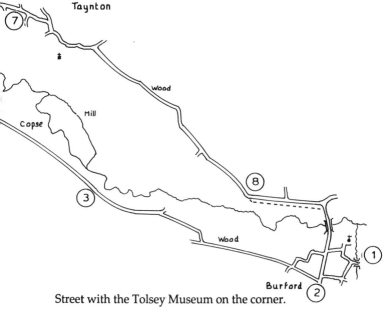

Street with the Tolsey Museum on the corner.

2. Turn right into Sheep Street and head out of Burford, passing the Bay Tree Hotel then the Lamb Inn. After about ³/₄ of a mile you will reach a lane that crosses the road; to the left is a small chapel and burial ground. Turn right into the lane, follow it

127

The rabbits are plentiful around Great Barrington

round and pass a group of cottages at right angles to the lane.

3. On your left the land rises gently while to the right, the land dips down to the Windrush. The village of Taynton is visible on higher ground on the opposite bank. As the lane and river curve slightly to the left, the village of Great Barrington can be seen ahead but across the river.

4. Continue ahead passing Barrington Riding School (left), and soon after, the small village church (right). On reaching the junction at Little Barrington, turn left, then right with the open green (right) until you reach the old water pump.

5. At the pump turn right and go down the village street with the green (right) and at the end of the cottages, and on joining the road, turn left. At the next road junction, bear right past The Fox Inn, cross the two branches of the River Windrush using Strong's Causeway then climb the hill into Great Barrington.

6. At the war memorial turn right and walk down the main street between the severe looking houses

Little Barrington

of this rather gaunt village, leaving the village by passing a large barn (right) converted to a private dwelling. The river and its attendant water meadows become apparent on the right.

7. Continue along the road through the attractive hamlet of Taynton, to Burford.

8. Immediately before the junction with the A424 (left), cross the stile into the field (right), where the right of way is indicated by the arrow. Continue ahead keeping the hedge to your left and staying left of the river, until you reach the bottom of the High Street.

Over the stone stile and back to Burford

Places and Points of Interest Along the Way

THE BARRINGTONS and TAYNTON

Little Barrington is a picturesque village of cottages surrounding the large, undulating village green where goats graze and ducks glide in the brook. To the east of the village is the Church of St Peter, where some of the stone work is Norman, including the doorway and the arches of the nave arcade.

In almost complete contrast to its little neighbour is the architecture of Great Barrington just across the causeway. Here the village appears to be rather dilapidated and unkept. But St Mary's, next to Barrington Park, is a light and airy church which has an original Norman chancel arch and contains several monuments to the Talbot family who bought Barrington Park in 1734.

One of the most famous sons of the Barringtons was Thomas Strong, who was considered by Wren to be one of the finest of English masons. He was employed as a leading mason on the

The Fox Inn

The Tolsey, Burford

building of St Paul's Cathedral, the foundation stone of which was laid by him. The honour of laying the last stone, however, fell to his brother Edward who succeeded him as Master Mason of England on his death.

In his will, Thomas Strong left money "to make a way between Barrington Bridges that two men may go a front to carry a corpse in safety", hence the name Strong's Causeway given to the road that links the two villages.

Overlooking the water meadows of the Windrush valley and lying closer to Burford is the quiet village of Taynton which became famous for its stone. Christopher Wren used it for St Paul's Cathedral and other London churches. It was also used for many Oxford colleges and 200,000 tonnes of it for the building of Blenheim Palace.

Taynton

18: *Chedworth Woods, Withington, Chedworth Roman Villa*

Map Landranger:	163
Start:	GR: SP 039 127
Distance:	5³/₄ miles

This walk follows a circuit close to the famous Roman Villa, through Chedworth Woods and along the Coln valley to Withington. The Mill Inn with its large garden around the mill stream is a good place to 'tarry awhile' before continuing along the banks of the River Coln and returning to the start along woodland paths.

In springtime primroses grow in great profusion in Chedworth Woods

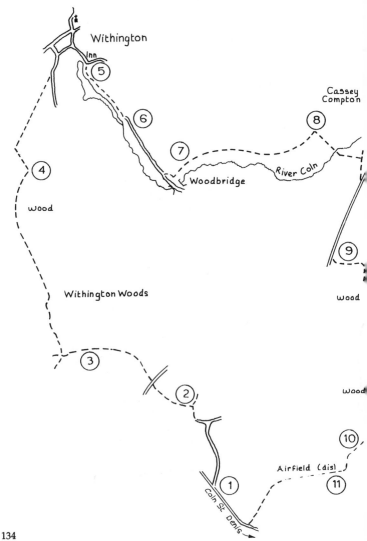

Route

1. At the old airfield, turn up the road signposted Compton Adale and then park in the lay-by on the right. Walk along the road in the same direction and where the road bends sharply to the right, turn left on to a concrete track taking the path to the right of the metal gate.

2. On entering the wood, go left and walk keeping the wall and fence on your left until reaching a stile (left). Cross into the field, turning sharp right and continuing until reaching the road. Cross the road and enter the track to Woodlands Farm. Pass through the metal gate, following the track down and into the woods.

3. Pass the cottage (left) and continue until the track enters a clearing. Take the second track (right) up the hill with a high wire fence on your left. Follow this track round to the right between wire fences and at the junction take the third track right. Soon the track drops down through two metal gates to fields below.

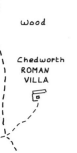

Wood

Chedworth
ROMAN
VILLA

4. After leaving the woods, turn immediately left passing through the gate and into the field. Walk ahead keeping the woods on the left until the right of way markers just before the overhead pylons indicate the route diagonally left across the fields to the stile at the bottom of the field. At the road go left, taking the first right on entering Withington, then right again towards the Mill Inn.

5. Across the road from the Mill Inn, the right of way goes across the yard, up a flight of steps and to the left of a cottage. Follow the right of way sign. Cross the stile and continue along the river bank, crossing a second stile before passing to the left of a cottage.

6. At the road, go right and look for the footpath sign indicating the right of way (left) under the former railway bridge at Woodbridge. On the other side of the old railway embankment, turn right down the track, then cross the stile (left) before

The Mill Inn, Withington

reaching the river bridge. Cross the field behind the house and enter the adjoining field via a metal gate.

7. The path continues through woods and meadows with the river on the right, passes through a stone wall and over a stile with a waymarker and metal gate. Enter the field (right) and go to the next stile. After crossing go down the field, over the footbridge and then left over the next stile.

8. At the gate join the track and bear right up the hill, between the two large trees with farm buildings to the left. Cross the stile onto the road, turning right to climb the hill and after passing the nature reserve, turn left off the road at the yellow way marker.

9. Follow the path down through the woods until a junction of tracks is reached. To visit the Chedworth Roman Villa, turn left down the hill. To continue the walk, turn right and climb to the top of the hill.

10. Turn left, then immediately right to walk into a field, leaving the woods behind. At the disused airfield, bear left along the wire fence.

11. Follow the "third runway", following it round left until a road is reached. At the road, turn right then right again at the Compton Abdale sign thence to return to the starting point.

Places and Points of Interest Along the Way

WITHINGTON

Close to the head of the Coln Valley and partly enclosed by woodland is the village of Withington. It is a pleasant village with a sixteenth-century rectory, a seventeenth-century manor house, a collection of attractive cottages and an old school house up on the hill near the Church of St Michael. As is frequently so in the Cotswolds, the church has Norman doorways, the south door being particularly elaborate. Inside the walls have unfortunately been damaged but the monument to Sir John Howe, who lived at the seventeenth-century mansion of Cassey Compton with his wife and eight children, is quite unusual.

CHEDWORTH ROMAN VILLA

The first signs that there were Roman remains in Chedworth Woods was in 1864 when a gamekeeper spotted Roman building debris and small pieces of mosaic which had been thrown up by rabbits whilst digging their burrows. Twelve months later the land, owned by the Earl of Eldon, was excavated and in 1924 was passed to the National Trust. The remains of other villas have been located quite close by at Yanworth, Withington and Bibury but Chedworth is amongst the finest in Britain. It was clearly a very large house with thirty-two rooms and separate bath houses. The floor layout of the villa, including its very intricate mosaic work, is exposed for all to see and the small museum at the site houses a collection of objects found during the excavations.

The mosaic floors of the Warm Room at Chedworth Roman Villa

19: Coln St Dennis, Fossebridge, Chedworth

Map Landranger:	163
Start:	GR: SP 085 113
Distance:	4 miles

Our route takes us up from the flat fields of Coln St Dennis, across the busy Fosse Way at Fossebridge and along the river banks up to the picturesque village of Chedworth where the sixteenth-century

The Norman church at Coln St Dennis

Three Tuns Inn is well worth a stop for lunch. After passing through the village fine views can be enjoyed before making a descent of Pancake Hill to rejoin the river for the return to Coln St Dennis.

Route

1. Park near the telephone box at Coln St Dennis. Walk through the village passing the church (left), cross the bridge over the River Coln and where the road bends left go straight ahead up the track.

2. At the signpost (right) go through the metal gate into a field and walk slightly diagonally left following the markers to the bottom left of the field. Pass through the metal gate, walk down the field towards Fossebridge Inn ahead and cross the stile onto the road.

3. Turn left, cross the road and just past the cottages on the right follow the unmarked trackway into the field. Walk towards the bank of trees ahead, go left and follow the path with the trees and hedges (right), further right is the River Coln.

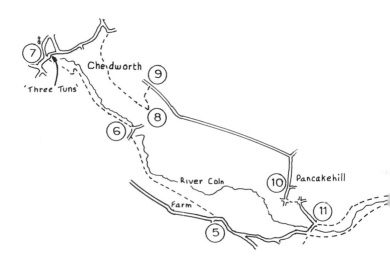

*The Three Tuns,
Chedworth*

4. At the bottom of the field pass through a gate and walk with the river on the right, now little more than a stream, until you reach the road. Cross the stile and turn left along the road. Pass the sign to Chedworth (left), with telephone box (right), continue

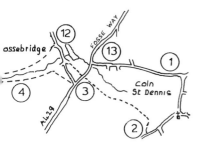

to a house on right called Saffron Hill where the right of way is to the left of the house.

5. Walk down the track, cross the stile into the field and after crossing the next two fields via gates and a further two fields via stiles, finally reach the road. Turn right, walk down the hill and go left opposite Brook Cottage into

141

Buttressed houses at steeply terraced Chedworth

the field with the stream right and enter a small coppice.

6. Cross a stone stile then a series of further stiles to cross the fields with the river (right). On reaching an equestrian centre, with a row of cottages up the hill (right) turn left over a stile, cross the disused railway and immediately turn right over a stone stile into a field. Go diagonally left and onto the road with the sixteenth-century public house The Three Tuns on the right.

7. Turn right, walk down past The Three Tuns, through the village and climb the hill bearing round to the right at the top. Where the road turns left take the track right via the gateway. With a stone wall on the right, follow the track round as it bears left and climb over a stile. Continue straight ahead between the houses, through a gate, a stile and second gate.

8. At the lane turn left, go through the gateway ahead with house right and climb up the field exiting at the top left over two stiles and a further field and stile.

9. At the track turn right, follow it and at the crossing of the tracks continue ahead until you reach the fork and go right.

10. At Green Hill Farm (right) cross the road, take the track opposite and where the track curves right, go left through the metal gate just past the house. Walk straight ahead on the path until you reach a crossing, turn left and when the road is reached go right past the Old Manse and descend the hill.

11. At the bottom of the hill the right of way, a grass pathway goes straight ahead between Orchard Cottage and Badger Cottage, then crosses a stile into a field and continues alongside the remains of a stone wall (right). Pass through a wooden gate. At first walk alongside the river, then the right of way gradually climbs away from the river towards a stile on the left, with a pylon below right.

12. Cross the stile into the field and exit via the metal gate onto the road. Turn right and walk until you reach a public footpath sign left. Follow the footpath with the wall, River Coln and a fence (right). At the road with the Fossebridge Inn (left), turn left and walk along the road (A429) Fosse Way.

Winter at Chedworth

13. At the sign to Coln St Dennis turn right down the lane and retrace your steps back to the phone box.

Places and Points of Interest Along the Way

COLN ST DENNIS

Living close to the river bearing the same name as their suffix are the villages of St Aldwyns, Rogers and St Dennis. Coln St Dennis, formerly owned by the Abbey of St Dennis, Paris is little more than a huddle of houses and cottages amidst the flat farmland at the

The right of way between Orchard Cottage and Badger Cottage

Water splashes down at the roadside on its way to the River Coln at the bottom of Chedworth village

rivers edge. It is most noted for its almost unspoilt Norman church which was built some 70 years after the Battle of Hastings.

It is quite remarkable that this little church has retained many of its original characteristics over the centuries. The Norman layout of the sanctuary, central tower and nave are unaltered but some alterations were made during later years, these being a belfry to the short squat tower and a porch to the north door. The tower, still standing after 850 years is unique in the Cotswolds, most other churches of this layout have long since lost their central towers. In the church is a memorial dated 1631 to Joan Burton that reads: "Hear lyes my body fast inclosed within this watery ground; by my precious soule it cannot nowe be founde."

During 1975 a flint knife with excellent cutting blade was found in a garden in Coln St Dennis. After study at the Ashmolean Museum in Oxford, it was established that it dated from the Neolithic period or the New Stone Age, thereby indicating that colonisation took place along the Coln many centuries before the Normans built their church there.

CHEDWORTH
Straggling around the steep, terraced hillside the village of Chedworth commands fine views across the gurgling stream that hurries down past buttressed houses to join the River Coln below. The whole village slopes up and down, being built on many different levels and at many various angles.

20: Sheepscombe, Cranham

Map Landranger:	163
Start:	GR: SO 892 102
Distance:	5¹/₄ miles

This route takes us from the wooded valley bottom at Sheepscombe up to the extensive common land above the steep-sided valley at Cranham. Initially the going is steep and during wet weather the right of way can be muddy. This walk can be made any time of the year but as much of it passes through woodland the autumn colours can be quite spectacular and as good hostelries exist in both villages the walker is spoilt for choice.

Route

1. At Sheepscombe park by the Church of St John the Apostle, turn right down the hill and then left at the war memorial where the road is signposted to Painswick.

2. Cross the stream at the bottom of the hill to pass between the village hall and the new post office (right) and the old post office at Coldstream Cottage (left).

The Black Horse, Cranham

Sheepscombe with the old Post Office, left

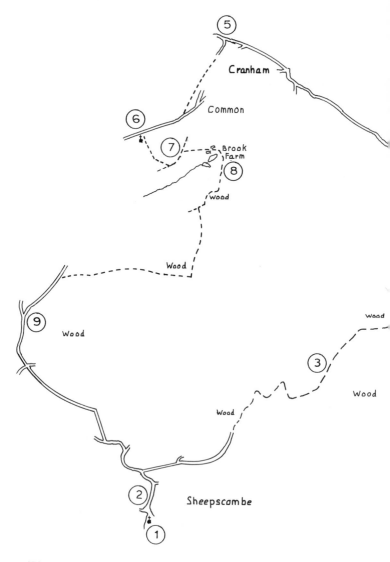

Climb up the hill, turn right at the Butcher's Arms and continue down the lane signposted Far Sheepscombe until Far End House is reached. Take the track (right) at the sign "National Trust - Workmans' Wood" where the right of way is indicated with blue arrow markers.

3. Pass the small stone barn with a metal roof (right) and continue straight ahead on the bridleway indicated with blue arrow markers. Continue walking straight ahead, past the next two crossings until the end of the wood is reached. Pass through a metal gate with a National Trust sign (right), climb the track to a further gate, exiting right of Ebworth Farmhouse and turn left onto the footpath that runs parallel to the road.

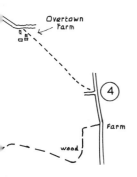

4. Soon you must join the road for a short distance, until the blue arrow markers indicate the bridleway left running diagonally at about 45° to the road towards the farm ahead. Skirt round to the right of the metal farm buildings, join the road at Overtown Farm and turn left following the road down in Cranham.

5. Pass the village hall on the left. Lower down the hill at Greensleeves and Brookefield (right), turn left passing Cranham House left, towards The Black Horse (left). Continue up the track, over the common and turn right at the road. Pass the village school (left), soon the village church will be reached (left).

6. The right of way passes through the churchyard to the left of the church and exits via a wooden kissing gate onto a pathway with a tall hedge (left) and wire fence (right). Cross the lane and continue along the path until a metal gate is reached, pass through it and into the woods. At the junction of the paths turn left and climb the hill emerging on the track just above Brook Farm Trout Fisheries.

7. Turn right down the track taking the path left just before the Fisheries is reached. Skirt round the buildings (right) and

Far End House, right, beyond is Workmans' Wood

when the lakes are reached take the bridleway through the gateway (left) and enter the National Nature Reserve, Saltridge.

8. Climb the hill and at the next junction of the tracks take the extreme left indicated by the blue arrow marker on the tree (right). Climb upwards again until a drystone wall with farmland beyond is reached at the next junction of the tracks. Take the track which is first right and go down the hill. When the end of Saltridge Woods is reached continue down the track ahead as indicated by the blue arrow marker. Pass through a wooden gate and turn left along the surfaced lane.

The Butcher's Arms, Sheepscombe

Places and Points of Interest Along the Way

SHEEPSCOMBE and CRANHAM

The small hamlet of Sheepscombe lies at the head of the Painswick Valley, scattered along both banks of the stream that flows down the valley to Painswick. The village itself is most picturesque, being set out at many different levels with the more modern houses blending in well with the older buildings including the tiny post office and the Butchers Arms public house.

It seems that prior to the early 1800s there was little here to recommend the place to anyone, the 700 or so villagers were rough, ignorant and poor people with neither school nor church. Sheepscombe did, however, have a number of well used ale houses, consequently there was much drunkenness amongst the inhabitants who in the main relied for their livelihood on Wright's Mill. The small Victorian Church of St John the Apostle with its unusual tower, often referred to as a turret, was consecrated early in 1820 after less than a year's construction and together with the opening of a school, the village's future prospects were improved.

Cranham sits in the middle of extensive beech woods which are generally accepted as being amongst the finest in the country, whilst many of its cottages are scattered about the large area of hilly common land. The small Church of St James the Great dates from the fifteenth century but in recent times has been subject to extensive renovation. An acknowledgement of the village's former source of wealth is indicated by the carvings of two sets of sheep shears, one below the other and to the left of the mid-section of the gargoyled tower. From the churchyard itself, with its well clipped yew trees, fine views can be seen across the surrounding heavily wooded and steep sided valleys.

The stone footbridge, Lower Slaughter. (Walk 4)

CICERONE GUIDES

Cicerone publish a wide range of reliable guides to walking and climbing abroad

FRANCE
TOUR OF MONT BLANC
CHAMONIX MONT BLANC - A Walking Guide
TOUR OF THE OISANS: GR54
WALKING THE FRENCH ALPS: GR5
THE CORSICAN HIGH LEVEL ROUTE: GR20
THE WAY OF ST JAMES: GR65
THE PYRENEAN TRAIL: GR10
THE RLS (Stevenson) TRAIL
TOUR OF THE QUEYRAS
ROCK CLIMBS IN THE VERDON
WALKS IN VOLCANO COUNTRY (Auvergne)
WALKING THE FRENCH GORGES (Provence)
FRENCH ROCK

FRANCE / SPAIN
WALKS AND CLIMBS IN THE PYRENEES
ROCK CLIMBS IN THE PYRENEES

SPAIN
WALKS & CLIMBS IN THE PICOS DE EUROPA
WALKING IN MALLORCA
BIRDWATCHING IN MALLORCA
COSTA BLANCA CLIMBS
ANDALUSIAN ROCK CLIMBS
THE WAY OF ST JAMES

FRANCE / SWITZERLAND
THE JURA - Walking the High Route and
   Winter Ski Traverses
CHAMONIX TO ZERMATT The Walker's
   Haute Route

SWITZERLAND
WALKING IN THE BERNESE ALPS
CENTRAL SWITZERLAND
WALKS IN THE ENGADINE
WALKING IN TICINO
THE VALAIS - A Walking Guide
THE ALPINE PASS ROUTE

GERMANY / AUSTRIA / EASTERN EUROPE
THE KALKALPEN TRAVERSE
KLETTERSTEIG - Scrambles
WALKING IN THE BLACK FOREST
MOUNTAIN WALKING IN AUSTRIA
WALKING IN THE HARZ MOUNTAINS
WALKING IN THE SALZKAMMERGUT
KING LUDWIG WAY
HUT-TO-HUT IN THE STUBAI ALPS
THE HIGH TATRAS

ITALY & SLOVENIA
ALTA VIA - High Level Walks in the Dolomites
VIA FERRATA - Scrambles in the Dolomites
ITALIAN ROCK - Rock Climbs in Northern Italy
CLASSIC CLIMBS IN THE DOLOMITES
WALKING IN THE DOLOMITES
THE JULIAN ALPS

MEDITERRANEAN COUNTRIES
THE MOUNTAINS OF GREECE
CRETE: Off the beaten track
TREKS & CLIMBS IN WADI RUM, JORDAN
THE ATLAS MOUNTAINS
WALKS & CLIMBS IN THE ALA DAG (Turkey)

OTHER COUNTRIES
ADVENTURE TREKS - W. N. AMERICA
ADVENTURE TREKS - NEPAL
ANNAPURNA TREKKERS GUIDE
CLASSIC TRAMPS IN NEW ZEALAND
TREKKING IN THE CAUCAUSUS

GENERAL OUTDOOR BOOKS
THE HILL WALKERS MANUAL
FIRST AID FOR HILLWALKERS
MOUNTAIN WEATHER
MOUNTAINEERING LITERATURE
THE ADVENTURE ALTERNATIVE
MODERN ALPINE CLIMBING
ROPE TECHNIQUES IN MOUNTAINEERING
MODERN SNOW & ICE TECHNIQUES
LIMESTONE -100 BEST CLIMBS IN BRITAIN

CANOEING
SNOWDONIA WILD WATER, SEA & SURF
WILDWATER CANOEING
CANOEIST'S GUIDE TO THE NORTH EAST

CARTOON BOOKS
ON FOOT & FINGER
ON MORE FEET & FINGERS
LAUGHS ALONG THE PENNINE WAY

*Also a full range of guidebooks
to walking, scrambling, ice-climbing,
rock climbing, and other adventurous
pursuits in Britain and abroad*

*Other guides are constantly being added to the Cicerone List.
Available from bookshops, outdoor equipment shops or direct (send for price list)
from CICERONE, 2 POLICE SQUARE, MILNTHORPE, CUMBRIA, LA7 7PY*

CICERONE GUIDES

Cicerone publish a wide range of reliable guides to walking and climbing in Britain, and other general interest books.

LAKE DISTRICT - General Books
A DREAM OF EDEN
LAKELAND VILLAGES
LAKELAND TOWNS
REFLECTIONS ON THE LAKES
OUR CUMBRIA
THE HIGH FELLS OF LAKELAND
CONISTON COPPER A History
LAKELAND - A taste to remember (Recipes)
THE LOST RESORT? (Morecambe)
CHRONICLES OF MILNTHORPE
LOST LANCASHIRE (Furness area)
THE PRIORY OF CARTMEL

LAKE DISTRICT - Guide Books
CASTLES IN CUMBRIA
THE CUMBRIA CYCLE WAY
WESTMORLAND HERITAGE WALK
IN SEARCH OF WESTMORLAND
CONISTON COPPER MINES Field Guide
SCRAMBLES IN THE LAKE DISTRICT
MORE SCRAMBLES IN THE LAKE DISTRICT
SHORT WALKS - SOUTH LAKELAND
WINTER CLIMBS IN THE LAKE DISTRICT
WALKS IN SILVERDALE/ARNSIDE
BIRDS OF MORECAMBE BAY
THE EDEN WAY
WALKING ROUND THE LAKES

NORTHERN ENGLAND (outside the Lakes
BIRDWATCHING ON MERSEYSIDE
CANAL WALKS Vol 1 North
CANOEISTS GUIDE TO THE NORTH EAST
THE CLEVELAND WAY & MISSING LINK
THE DALES WAY
DOUGLAS VALLEY WAY
HADRIANS WALL Vol 1 The Wall Walk
HERITAGE TRAILS IN NW ENGLAND
THE ISLE OF MAN COASTAL PATH
IVORY TOWERS & DRESSED STONES (Follies)
THE LANCASTER CANAL
LANCASTER CANAL WALKS
LAUGHS ALONG THE PENNINE WAY
A NORTHERN COAST-TO-COAST
NORTH YORK MOORS Walks
THE REIVERS WAY (Northumberland)
THE RIBBLE WAY
ROCK CLIMBS LANCASHIRE & NW
THE YORKSHIRE DALES A walker's guide
WALKING IN THE SOUTH PENNINES
WALKING IN THE NORTH PENNINES
WALKS IN THE YORKSHIRE DALES (3 VOL)
WALKS IN LANCASHIRE WITCH COUNTRY
WALKS IN THE NORTH YORK MOORS
WALKS TO YORKSHIRE WATERFALLS (2 vol)
WALKS ON THE WEST PENNINE MOORS
WALKING NORTHERN RAILWAYS (2 vol)
WALKING IN THE WOLDS

DERBYSHIRE & EAST MIDLANDS
WHITE PEAK WALKS - 2 Vols
HIGH PEAK WALKS
WHITE PEAK WAY
KINDER LOG
THE VIKING WAY
THE DEVIL'S MILL / WHISTLING CLOUGH (Novels)

WALES & WEST MIDLANDS
THE RIDGES OF SNOWDONIA
HILLWALKING IN SNOWDONIA
HILL WALKING IN WALES (2 Vols)
ASCENT OF SNOWDON
WELSH WINTER CLIMBS
SNOWDONIA WHITE WATER SEA & SURF
SCRAMBLES IN SNOWDONIA
SARN HELEN Walking Roman Road
ROCK CLIMBS IN WEST MIDLANDS
THE SHROPSHIRE HILLS A Walker's Guide
HEREFORD & THE WYE VALLEY A Walker's Guide
THE WYE VALLEY WALK

SOUTH & SOUTH WEST ENGLAND
COTSWOLD WAY
EXMOOR & THE QUANTOCKS
THE KENNET & AVON WALK
THE SOUTHERN-COAST-TO-COAST
SOUTH DOWNS WAY & DOWNS LINK
SOUTH WEST WAY - 2 Vol
WALKING IN THE CHILTERNS
WALKING ON DARTMOOR
WALKERS GUIDE TO DARTMOOR PUBS
WALKS IN KENT
THE WEALDWAY & VANGUARD WAY

SCOTLAND
THE BORDER COUNTRY - WALKERS GUIDE
SCRAMBLES IN LOCHABER
SCRAMBLES IN SKYE
THE ISLAND OF RHUM
CAIRNGORMS WINTER CLIMBS
THE CAIRNGORM GLENS (Mountainbike Guide)
THE ATHOLL GLENS (Mountainbike Guide)
WINTER CLIMBS BEN NEVIS & GLENCOE
SCOTTISH RAILWAY WALKS
TORRIDON A Walker's Guide
SKI TOURING IN SCOTLAND

REGIONAL BOOKS UK & IRELAND
THE MOUNTAINS OF ENGLAND & WALES
    VOL 1 WALES VOL 2 ENGLAND
THE MOUNTAINS OF IRELAND
THE ALTERNATIVE PENNINE WAY
THE PACKHORSE BRIDGES OF ENGLAND
THE RELATIVE HILLS OF BRITAIN
LIMESTONE - 100 BEST CLIMBS

Also a full range of EUROPEAN and OVERSEAS guidebooks - walking, long distance trails, scrambling, ice-climbing, rock climbing.

Other guides are constantly being added to the Cicerone List.
Available from bookshops, outdoor equipment shops or direct (send s.a.e. for price list) from
CICERONE, 2 POLICE SQUARE, MILNTHORPE, CUMBRIA, LA7 7PY

Printed by CARNMOR PRINT & DESIGN,
95-97 LONDON ROAD, PRESTON, LANCASHIRE, UK.